RECIPE HALL OF FAME

Family
Favorites
COOKBOOK

Parmesan
Oven-Fried Chicken
page 104

RECIPE HALL OF FAME

Family Favorites
COOKBOOK

Edited by
Gwen McKee and Barbara Moseley

Photographs by Christian and Elise Stella

QUAIL RIDGE PRESS
Preserving America's Food Heritage

On the cover: Parmesan Oven-Fried Chicken, page 104, Bread Pot Fondue, page 19, and Banana-Pineapple Upside-Down Cake, page 138.

Printed in the United States of America

First edition

Library of Congress Cataloging-in-Publication Data

Recipe hall of fame family favorites cookbook / edited by Gwen McKee and Barbara Moseley.
　　pages cm.
　　"Preserving America's food heritage."
　　Includes index.
　　ISBN 978-1-934193-93-8
1. Cooking, American. 2. Cooking—Competitions—United States. I. McKee, Gwen. II. Moseley, Barbara. III. Title: Family favorites cookbook.
　　TX715.R2893 2013
　　641.5973—dc23　　　　　　　　　　　　　　2012048275

About the Photography:
The food photographs in this book were taken by Christian and Elise Stella. All food in the photographs was purchased at ordinary grocery stores and prepared exactly to recipe directions. No artificial food-styling techniques were used to enhance the food's appearance. Only water was sometimes spritzed on the food to keep it looking fresh during the photo shoot.

QUAIL RIDGE PRESS
P. O. Box 123 • Brandon, MS 39043
info@quailridge.com • www.quailridge.com
www.facebook.com/cookbookladies

Contents

Peanut Butter-Kiss Cookies page 157

Preface

$\mathcal{I}$ sincerely believe that most of our quality times together as a family are around a table of good food. This book is about presenting best-loved recipes that are easy to understand, follow, and prepare for your family.

My co-editor Barbara Moseley and I have spent most of our lives testing and developing recipes. Our spouses and children were, of course, our taste testers of recipes from whatever book we were working on at the time. Although a new favorite would often emerge, they were quick to remind us: "You haven't made lasagna in a while, Mom." Or, "When are we going to have chicken and dumplin's again?"

So, in order to find these family favorites, we went to our huge database of recipes in our BEST OF THE BEST STATE COOKBOOK SERIES, and found out what people from all over the country consistently said they liked best. In keeping with our motto, Preserving America's Food Heritage, we selected 220 tried-and-true recipes that we deem outstanding.

One criteria was efficiency. Some of the recipes we selected have been somebody's family favorites for a long time, and have procedures that may seem a little old-fashioned. So we give you Editor's Extras suggesting shortcuts and substitutions to make it even easier, and perhaps even better.

Our other consideration was expense. In choosing these recipes, we have endeavored to keep the cost of ingredients reasonable . . . with a few exceptions, when splurging on your family is just the right thing to do.

Today's busy schedules seem to make it difficult for the family to be together at one time for dinner. But if you plan ahead, and announce what family favorite you are serving tonight, chances are they will make the extra effort to be there. I guarantee you will be doing the most for the entire family with the simple gesture of cooking a meal they all love. Ask for their help, and don't hesitate to exchange cooking instructions and ideas—and recipes—with them!

Our annual family beach trip in mid-summer, when we find a week we can all gather from Oregon, Massachusetts, and Mississippi, is full of recipe occasions. We have teams of "chefs du jour" who come up with a dinner menu and theme of their choice, complete with decorations for their special night. Invariably, the meals are built around or include a family favorite. One might start their Oriental Escapade with Chinese Chicken Wings (page 15), or prepare a big Caesar Salad (page 41) for an Italian Rendezvous, or serve Cajun Red Beans and Rice (page 63) for a Louisiana Fais Do Do, or Key Lime Cheese-

Granddaughters Eva and Olivia are beginning to offer their own dishes to the Mexican night dinner menu.

cake (page 150) to end an Evening in the Tropics. It is a treasured family tradition now, and we all get quite excited about making our night the most memorable and fun.

We are grateful to Christian and Elise Stella for their lovely photographs, and to all those wonderful cooks all over America for sharing their recipes. Because we always like to give you interesting and fun things to read, we have included inspirational, family, and food quotes, dinner conversation suggestions, and even a few jokes along with our tips and Editor's Extras.

Whether you are an experienced cook, or tackling it for the first time, cooking is really quite simple—anybody can do it—you just have to want to, or be hungry enough! Turn the pages to find a tempting recipe that beckons you to give it a try. The results will have you coming back for more.

This may indeed become your "go-to" cookbook. We hope it inspires you to create and re-create favorite family recipes for years to come.

Gwen McKee

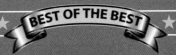

Nibbles & Snacks

Taffy Apple Dip

"An apple a day keeps the doctor away." What a great dip for apples! Make this for after-school apple snacks.

1 (8-ounce) package cream
  cheese, softened
¾ cup brown sugar
¼ cup sugar
1 tablespoon vanilla extract

Chopped honey-glazed nuts for
  garnish
Assorted unpeeled apple slices,
  sprinkled with lemon juice

Mix cream cheese, sugars, and vanilla, blending well; chill. Before serving, sprinkle nuts on top. Serve with apple wedges.

From Chaney Creek to the Chesapeake (Virginia)

Most Requested Men's Dip

Treat your family and guests to an absolutely delicious dip. Serve with thin wheat crackers, and watch it disappear. (Women love it, too!)

1 (8-ounce) package cream
  cheese, softened
1 (8-ounce) carton sour cream
2 (.75-ounce) packages dry
  Italian salad dressing mix

2 (4½-ounce) cans tiny shrimp,
  drained
2 tablespoons lemon juice
½ green bell pepper, finely
  minced

Combine all ingredients. Allow the flavors to blend for awhile (a day, if possible) prior to serving. Serve with thin wheat crackers. Makes about 2½ cups.

Taste Buds (North Carolina)

The family is the nucleus of civilization.
—Ariel and Will Durant

Avocado-Crab Dip

This dip is always the first to disappear.

1 large avocado, diced
1 tablespoon fresh lemon
   juice
2 tablespoons grated onion
1 tablespoon Worcestershire

4 ounces cream cheese, softened
½ cup sour cream
½ teaspoon salt
1 (7½-ounce) can crabmeat,
   drained and flaked

Use a firm avocado to avoid a messy-looking dip, and toss, rather than mix, with lemon juice, onion, and Worcestershire. Stir in cream cheese, sour cream, and salt. Add crabmeat, and fold carefully into seasoned avocado. Serve with tortilla chips or crackers.

Editor's Extra: If you choose to splurge on refrigerated fresh crabmeat, all the better.

Pupus–An Island Tradition (Hawaii)

Layered Nacho Dip

The dip that never fails to win most popular.

1 pound lean ground beef
1 (16-ounce) can refried beans
1 (1¼-ounce) package taco
   seasoning mix
1 (6-ounce) carton avocado dip
1 (8-ounce) carton sour cream
1 (4½-ounce) can chopped
   ripe olives, drained

2 large tomatoes, chopped,
   drained
1 small onion, finely chopped
1 (4-ounce) can chopped green
   chiles, drained
3 cups shredded Monterey Jack
   cheese

Cook beef until thoroughly browned. Drain off all grease. Add beans and taco seasoning; mix well. When cooled, spread into a 9x13-inch glass dish. Layer all remaining ingredients (in order listed) over beef mixture; chill. Serve with Doritos or corn chips. Keeps several days.

Sisters' Secrets (Louisiana)

BLT Bites

BLT Bites

These little babies have become classic buffet favorites, and with good reason.

16–20 cherry tomatoes
1 pound bacon, cooked and
  crumbled
½ cup mayonnaise or salad
  dressing

⅓ cup chopped green onions
3 tablespoons grated Parmesan
  cheese
2 tablespoons snipped fresh
  parsley

Cut a thin slice off the top of each tomato. Scoop out and discard pulp. Invert tomatoes on a paper towel to drain.

In a small bowl, combine all remaining ingredients; mix well. Spoon into tomatoes. Refrigerate for several hours. Makes 16–20 appetizers.

Dutch Pantry Cookin' Volume II (West Virginia)

Hot Potato Skins

Potato skins need not be peeled and discarded—here they are spruced up to be the star of the show. Bravo!

Bake potatoes until tender. Cool, cut in quarters lengthwise, then in half crosswise, to form 8 sections. Scoop out potato pulp, leaving about ¼ inch. Brush skins on both sides with melted butter and a little soy sauce. Bake at 500° until crisp, 10–12 minutes. Serve with assorted dips, or add shredded cheese and crumbled, cooked bacon, then heat until cheese melts.

Editor's Extra: Use the scooped-out potato pulp for supper mashed potatoes, and the skins as a before-dinner treat.

Red River Valley Potato Growers Auxiliary Cookbook (Great Plains)

What can you do to promote world peace? Go home and love your family.
                                                        —Mother Teresa

Bacon-Wrapped Shrimp

Nice nibbles before a cookout.

1 (16-ounce) package bacon
40 large shrimp, peeled,
   deveined

1 (10-ounce) bottle teriyaki
   sauce

Cut each bacon slice in half. Wrap one piece of bacon around each shrimp, and secure with a wooden pick. Place in 9x13-inch baking dish. Pour teriyaki sauce over shrimp. Chill, covered, one hour. Bake at 400° for 10–15 minutes or until bacon is crisp. Serves 20.

Editor's Extra: May sub chili sauce for teriyaki sauce.

Beyond Cotton Country (Alabama)

Ham Spread

1 (8-ounce) tub soft-style cream
   cheese with chives and onion
½ teaspoon Dijon mustard
1 tablespoon mayonnaise

⅓ cup finely chopped, fully
   cooked ham
¼ cup shredded Cheddar cheese
Crackers, bread, or celery sticks

In a small mixing bowl, stir together cream cheese, mustard, and mayonnaise. Stir in ham and Cheddar cheese. Cover, and chill. Serve with crackers, bread, or celery sticks. Store leftover spread in the refrigerator, covered, for up to 5 days. Makes enough spread for 6 slices of bread.

Variations: To make roast beef spread, substitute cooked roast beef for the ham, and Swiss cheese for the Cheddar. To make turkey spread, substitute cooked turkey for the ham, and mozzarella cheese for the Cheddar.

Lion House Entertaining (Utah)

All great change in America begins at the dinner table.
—Ronald Reagan

Chinese Chicken Wings

Party food? Yes, but try serving it to your family for supper with some cole-slaw and baked beans. They'll love it!

3 garlic cloves, minced
1 small onion, minced
3 tablespoons chopped
   fresh parsley
1 cup soy sauce
½ cup vegetable oil

1 tablespoon Dijon mustard
1 tablespoon honey (or
   ½ tablespoon sugar)
3–5 pounds chicken wings,
   disjointed

Mix thoroughly in food processor or with wire whisk the garlic, onion, parsley, soy sauce, oil, mustard, and honey. Marinate wings for several hours at room temperature or overnight, covered in refrigerator.

Bake wings on a cookie sheet or jellyroll pan at 300° for 45 minutes, turning once, and broil for approximately 5 minutes or until wings are brown and bubbly.

A Taste of Salt Air & Island Kitchens (New England)

Oven Chicken Nuggets

This is great as a snack, but, like the wings, so popular you'll want to make a whole meal around them.

4 boneless, skinless chicken
   breasts
¼ cup grated Parmesan cheese
4 tablespoons grated Cheddar
   cheese
½ cup bread crumbs

1 teaspoon thyme
1 teaspoon basil
1 teaspoon salt
⅛ teaspoon pepper
½ cup melted butter or
   margarine

Cut chicken into 1-inch squares. Combine Parmesan cheese, Cheddar cheese, bread crumbs, thyme, basil, salt, and pepper; blend well. Dip chicken pieces into melted butter; roll in crumb mixture. Arrange chicken in a single layer on foil-lined baking sheets. Bake at 400° for 10 minutes. Serves 4–6.

What's Cookin' (Mid-Atlantic)

Hanky-Panky

A tasty, hearty snack.

1 pound ground beef
1 pound sausage
1 pound Velveeta, chopped
  or grated
1 tablespoon oregano

1 tablespoon Worcestershire
1 teaspoon garlic powder
1 loaf party rye bread

In skillet, brown beef and sausage together. Drain. Add remaining ingredients, except rye bread, and mix well. Heat until cheese is melted, stirring often. Spread on slices of rye bread, and place on baking sheet. Bake at 350° for 10 minutes.

Editor's Extras: Also good on French bread rounds, or as a dip with Frito Scoops.

Educated Taste (Georgia)

Sausage Balls

These delicious little gems have been elevated to a new taste level. Oh yeah!

1 pound sausage
1 green bell pepper, chopped
  fine
1 small onion, chopped fine

1 pound sharp Cheddar cheese,
  grated
3–4 cups Bisquick

Combine sausage, bell pepper, onion, and cheese. Mix until not sticky, adding Bisquick gradually. Knead, then roll into bite-size balls. Place on ungreased cookie sheet, and bake at 350° for about 6 minutes. Turn over, and bake on other side for about 3 minutes.

Dine with the Angels (Oklahoma)

You don't choose your family. They are God's gift to you, as you are to them.
—Desmond Tutu

Margaret's Tangy Meatballs

Get some family help rolling the meatballs—while you make the sauce. That makes them all the better. These are devilishly good.

MEATBALLS:

1 cup crushed cornflakes
2 pounds ground chuck
2 tablespoons onion flakes
2 tablespoons soy sauce
½ teaspoon pepper

½ teaspoon garlic powder
Dash of salt
2 eggs
½ cup ketchup

Mix all ingredients together, and form small Meatballs about the size of a quarter. Place in one layer in large baking pan.

SAUCE:

1 (12-ounce) jar chili sauce
1 (16-ounce) can jellied
  cranberry sauce

2 tablespoons sugar
2 tablespoons lemon juice

Mix Sauce ingredients; pour over Meatballs. Bake uncovered in 400° oven for 35 minutes. Serves 16–18. Meatballs may be made and frozen ahead of time.

A Samford Celebration Cookbook (Alabama)

The important thing is the family. If you can keep the family together—and that's the backbone of our whole business, catering to families—that's what we hope to do.
    —Walt Disney

Bread Pot Fondue

Bread Pot Fondue

This is great to make ahead and heat when you need it.

1 firm, round loaf of bread (1½ pounds, 8–10 inches in diameter)

Slice off top of bread loaf, reserving top. Hollow out inside of loaf with small paring knife, leaving ½-inch shell. Cut the removed bread into 1-inch cubes to serve later.

FILLING:

2 cups shredded mild Cheddar cheese	**1 (4-ounce) can chopped green chiles**
1 (8-ounce) package cream cheese, softened	**1 teaspoon Worcestershire**
1½ cups sour cream	**Assorted raw vegetables**
1 cup cooked, diced ham	**Cubed bread and crackers for dipping**
½ cup chopped green onions	

Combine cheeses and sour cream in bowl; stir in remaining ingredients except raw veggies and dippers. Spoon filling into hollowed loaf; replace top. Wrap loaf tightly with several layers of heavy-duty aluminum foil; set on cookie sheet. Bake at 350° for 70 minutes or until Filling is heated through. Remove from oven, and unwrap. Place on a platter and serve with fresh vegetables, cubed bread, and crackers.

Editor's Extra: Fun to melt a bag of chocolate chips in a small fondue pot or slow cooker, and serve with assorted fruit and cheese chunks alongside the bread bowl. My daughter does this for her teenagers and their friends, and you can guess where their favorite go-to place is. —*Gwen*

Country Classics II (Colorado)

To us, family means putting your arms around each other and being there.

—Barbara Bush

Fried Monterey Jack with Mexican Sauce

This sauce is fabulous no matter what you dip into it. But the cheese takes the prize.

MEXICAN SAUCE:

2 tablespoons peanut oil
⅓ cup sliced scallions
1 clove garlic, crushed
1 (15-ounce) can tomato sauce

2 tablespoons diced green chiles
2 teaspoons chili powder
½ teaspoon oregano leaves
¼ teaspoon ground cumin

Heat peanut oil in medium saucepan over medium heat. Sauté scallions and garlic until tender. Stir in tomato sauce, green chiles, chili powder, oregano, and cumin. Cover, and simmer 20 minutes, stirring occasionally. Makes about 2 cups.

CHEESE:

Peanut oil
2 (8-ounce) packages Monterey
   Jack cheese, cut in half
   crosswise and cut into
   ½-inch-thick slices

All-purpose flour
1 egg, beaten
1 cup finely rolled cracker crumbs
   or bread crumbs

In a large skillet or electric skillet, heat a 1-inch depth of peanut oil to 375°. Lightly coat cheese with flour. Dip in egg, then coat completely with cracker or bread crumbs. Fry cheese, a few pieces at a time, 30–60 seconds, or until crust is golden and centers are melted. Remove with slotted spoon; drain on paper towels. Serve immediately with Mexican Sauce. Makes about 16 pieces.

Editor's Extra: Try it with Pepper-Jack cheese for a cross between jalapeño poppers and mozzarella sticks.

Louisiana Largesse (Louisiana)

Never let 'em see you sweat. Guests feel guilty if they think you've worked too hard to make dinner for them—which, of course, you have!
—Ina Garten

McDade Cheese Muffins

Nice for a buffet brunch. Delicious any time.

1 (16-ounce) package ground
   sausage, cooked, drained
1 (11-ounce) can cheese soup

½ cup water
3 cups biscuit mix

Mix all together in a large bowl. Spoon into greased mini-muffin tins, and bake at 400° for 15 minutes. Makes 36 muffins.

Beyond the Grill (Mississippi)

Cheese Straws

A classic homemade treat that is ready to travel anywhere . . . to tailgates, picnic, in lunch boxes . . . and just as suitable on a buffet table.

1 stick butter, softened
½ pound grated sharp
   Cheddar cheese, softened
1½ cups all-purpose flour

1 teaspoon salt
½ teaspoon red pepper
Pecans halves (optional)
1 egg, beaten

Mix all ingredients, except pecans and egg, well. Roll into 1½-inch roll, about the diameter of a half-dollar; refrigerate. When cold, cut into ¼-inch slices. Place on ungreased cookie sheet; brush each slice with beaten egg, and place pecan half on top, if desired. Bake at 350° for 10–12 minutes; serve warm. Makes 3 dozen.

Note: Dough may be shaped over a stuffed olive and rolled into balls.

Editor's Extra: I like to roll dough to about ⅛-inch thinness, cut into strips, and place on cookie sheet. Bake at 250° for 45 minutes to 1 hour; turn oven off, but leave pan in oven till it cools. Makes a very crispy straw.—*Barbara*

Senator and Mrs. Wendell Ford of Kentucky
Seasons of Thyme (Kentucky)

A baby is God's opinion that the world should go on.
      —Carl Sandburg

Hugs and Kisses

Everyone LOVES this. You'll likely get a real hug and kiss for making it.

¼ cup butter or margarine, melted
1 tablespoon Worcestershire
1 teaspoon seasoned salt
1 cup pretzel sticks (bite-size lengths)
8 cups rice, corn, or wheat square cereal

Candy-coated chocolate candies, raisins, butterscotch morsels, miniature marshmallows, chocolate chips, or peanut butter morsels (optional)

Combine butter or margarine, Worcestershire, and seasoned salt, mixing well. Combine pretzels and cereal in large bowl. Drizzle seasoned butter over cereal mixture, and mix gently until evenly coated. Spread mixture in 10x14x3-inch baking pan. Bake at 300° for 1 hour, stirring at 15-minute intervals. Spread mixture on paper towels, and cool. Add 1 cup of one or mixed optional ingredients. Makes 10–12 cups.

Editor's Extra: Try subbing Cajun seasoning for the seasoned salt. Also good to add some sweet cereal to the mix, but not more than a 2-cup substitution.

Children's Party Book (Virginia)

Teddy Bear Snack Mix

Get the children to help with this family favorite . . . they'll enjoy making it and eating it, too.

3 cups teddy bear-shaped graham snacks
1 cup raisins
1 cup chopped dried apples

1 cup honey nut round toasted oat cereal
¼ cup candy-coated chocolate pieces (M&M type)

In a large bowl, mix graham snacks, raisins, dried apples, honey nut cereal, and chocolate pieces. Store in sealed plastic bag or airtight container at room temperature up to 5 days. Makes 12 (½-cup) servings.

Heart Smart Kids Cookbook (Michigan)

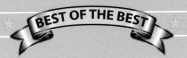
Bread & Breakfast

Mexican Cornbread

The perfect companion to any kind of greens. Yum!

½ pound hot sausage, cooked
½ cup all-purpose flour
3 teaspoons baking powder
2 teaspoons sugar
¾ teaspoon salt
1½ cups cornmeal

3 tablespoons butter, melted
¾ cup buttermilk
½ cup cream-style corn
½ cup chopped green chiles
1½ cups grated Cheddar cheese
1 egg, beaten

Combine all ingredients; mix well. Pour into a greased 9x13-inch pan. Bake at 350° for 30–40 minutes. Serves 10–12.

Our Daily Bread (West Virginia)

Shortcut Pepperoni Bread

Though good all by itself, this hearty bread goes really well with a luncheon salad. Who said pepperoni is for pizza only?

1 loaf frozen bread dough
½ pound Swiss cheese, sliced
½ pound pepperoni, thinly
  sliced

1 egg
Grated Parmesan cheese

Thaw dough according to package directions, and let rise. After dough has risen, cut in half; roll out each half as thinly as possible. Layer with Swiss cheese and pepperoni. Beat egg, and spread thinly over Swiss cheese and pepperoni. Sprinkle with Parmesan cheese. Roll into loaves. Bake at 350° for 30 minutes, or until golden brown. Makes 15 slices.

Philadelphia Homestyle Cookbook (Pennsylvania)

In every conceivable manner, the family is link to our past, bridge to our future.
—Alex Haley

Ranch Biscuits

2 cups biscuit mix
4 teaspoons dry ranch salad
   dressing mix
⅔ cup milk

2 tablespoons butter or
   margarine, melted
1 teaspoon dried parsley
⅛ teaspoon garlic powder

In a bowl, stir biscuit mix, salad dressing mix, and milk until combined. Drop by large spoonfuls 2 inches apart onto greased baking sheet. Bake at 425° for 10–15 minutes or until golden brown. In a small bowl, combine butter, parsley, and garlic powder; brush over warm biscuits. Makes 9 biscuits.

Mary B's Recipes (North Carolina)

Biscuits and Sausage Gravy

Even if you use frozen or canned biscuits, this is quick to make for hungry people who arrive in your kitchen ready to eat!

3 cups biscuit mix
¾ cup milk
½ pound pork sausage
½ stick butter or margarine

⅓ cup all-purpose flour
3½ cups milk
½ teaspoon salt
½ teaspoon pepper

Combine biscuit mix and milk; stir. On floured wax paper, roll dough to ¾-inch thickness; cut with biscuit cutter. Place on a greased baking sheet. Bake at 400° for 12–15 minutes or until golden.

For gravy, crumble and brown sausage in skillet. Drain, reserving 1 tablespoon drippings in skillet. Set sausage aside. Add butter to drippings; melt butter. Add flour, and cook 1 minute, stirring constantly. Gradually add milk; cook over medium heat, stirring constantly until thickened. Stir in seasonings and sausage. Cook until heated, stirring constantly. Serve sausage gravy over cooked biscuits. Serves 6–8.

Great Tastes of Texas (Texas)

Peach Upside Down Muffins

Peach Upside Down Muffins

You'll flip over these.

2 cups all-purpose flour
1½ cups sugar
1 tablespoon baking powder
½ teaspoon salt
¼ cup butter or butter-flavored shortening, melted
2 eggs, lightly beaten
1 cup milk
⅛ teaspoon cinnamon
½ teaspoon almond or vanilla extract
6 tablespoons butter or margarine, divided
1 cup plus 2 tablespoons packed brown sugar, divided
3 cups sliced, peeled, ripe peaches (or canned)

In a mixing bowl, combine flour, sugar, baking powder, and salt. Mix in butter, then eggs, milk, cinnamon, and extract; mix until smooth. In bottom of 18 greased muffin cups, place 1 teaspoon butter and 1 tablespoon brown sugar. Place in 375° oven for 2 minutes. Arrange peaches in the muffin cups. Fill each cup half full with batter. Bake at 375° for about 18 minutes or until browned. Turn out of pans immediately.

Heavenly Recipes (Great Plains)

Banana Muffins

Whip these up in no time, incorporating fruit and nuts into a dessert-like breakfast treat.

1 cup sugar
1 stick butter, softened
1 egg
½ cup sour cream
1 cup mashed ripe bananas
2 cups all-purpose flour
1 teaspoon vanilla
1 teaspoon baking soda
½ cup finely chopped nuts

Mix in order given. Fill greased muffin tins ¾ full. Bake at 350° for about 20 minutes.

Sharing our Best / Bergen Lutheran Church (Missouri)

Pineapple Nut Bread

A delicious alternative to banana nut bread.

2 cups all-purpose flour	2 eggs
1 tablespoon baking powder	⅔ cup milk
½ teaspoon salt	1 teaspoon vanilla
¼ teaspoon nutmeg	1 (8-ounce) can crushed
½ cup vegetable oil	pineapple, drained
¾ cup sugar	½ cup chopped pecans

Preheat oven to 350°. Sift flour, baking powder, salt, and nutmeg onto wax paper. In a large bowl, beat oil with sugar; add eggs, one at a time; mix well. Add dry ingredients alternately with milk. Stir in vanilla; add pineapple and pecans. Pour into a lightly greased and floured loaf pan. Bake 50 minutes. Cool completely before cutting.

Dd's Table Talk (Hawaii)

Banana-Pecan Coffee Cake

2 eggs	1½ cups all-purpose flour
½ cup shortening	¾ teaspoon salt
1½ cups sugar	1 cup chopped pecans
3 bananas, mashed	1 cup packed brown sugar
1 teaspoon vanilla extract	½ cup butter or margarine
1 teaspoon baking soda	1 (3-ounce) can flaked coconut
¼ cup buttermilk	

Beat eggs, shortening, sugar, bananas, and vanilla in mixer bowl until well blended. Add baking soda that has been dissolved in buttermilk; mix well. Add flour and salt; beat until well mixed. Stir in pecans. Pour into greased and floured 9x13-inch baking pan. Combine brown sugar, margarine, and coconut in saucepan. Cook over low heat until butter melts, stirring constantly. Spoon over batter. Bake at 350° for 45 minutes. Serves 15.

Editor's Extra: Many older recipes call for shortening rather than butter or margarine, but they are almost always interchangeable with similar baking results. The difference is in the taste.

Texas Accents (Texas)

Blueberry Coffee Cake

This delightful cake is indeed a winner. Prepare for the raves.

TOPPING:

½ cup granulated sugar   ½ stick cold butter
1 teaspoon ground cinnamon   ¼ cup chopped pecans (optional)

Combine sugar and cinnamon in small bowl. Cut in butter until mixture is crumbly. Refrigerate 30 minutes.

CAKE:

2 cups all-purpose flour   1 cup granulated sugar
1 teaspoon baking powder   2 eggs
1 teaspoon baking soda   1 cup sour cream
Dash of salt   1 teaspoon vanilla
1 stick butter or margarine,   2 cups fresh blueberries
  softened   (or frozen)

Preheat oven to 350°. Grease a 9x13-inch baking pan. Sift together flour, baking powder, baking soda, and salt. Set aside. Beat together butter and sugar in large bowl. Add eggs, sour cream, and vanilla; mix well. Add dry ingredients; mix well. Fold in blueberries. Pour into prepared pan. Sprinkle Topping mixture over batter. Bake at 350° for 40–45 minutes. Serves 8–10.

Winners (Indiana)

I went to a restaurant that said, "Breakfast anytime." So I ordered eggs during the Renaissance.
—Steven Wright

Quick Crescent Caramel Rolls

Quick Crescent Caramel Rolls

Your kids will love you for making these.

8 tablespoons butter or
  margarine, divided
¾ cup packed brown sugar
¼ cup water
½ cup chopped pecans
  (optional)

2 (8-ounce) cans refrigerated
  crescent dinner rolls
¼ cup sugar
2 teaspoons cinnamon

Preheat oven to 375°. In ungreased 9x13-inch baking dish, melt 5 tablespoons butter in oven. Stir in brown sugar, water, and pecans, if desired. Set aside. Separate each can of dough into 4 rectangles. Pinch perforations together to seal. Spread with 3 tablespoons softened butter. Combine sugar and cinnamon; sprinkle over dough. Starting at shorter side, roll up each rectangle. Cut each roll into 4 slices, making 32 pieces. Place cut-side down in prepared pan. Bake 20–25 minutes, until golden brown. Invert immediately to remove from pan. Serve warm. Makes 32 rolls.

Hint: To reheat, wrap in foil and warm at 350° for 10–15 minutes.

Editor's Extra: Nice to drizzle a little powdered sugar glaze on top.

Homecoming (Texas)

School Day Biscuits

How can anything so simple be so good?

½ cup packed brown sugar
1 teaspoon ground cinnamon
1 (12-ounce) can refrigerated
  buttermilk biscuits

¼ cup butter or margarine,
  melted

In small bowl, combine brown sugar and cinnamon. Separate biscuits; dip top of each in melted butter, then in cinnamon-sugar mixture. Place sugared-side-up on ungreased baking sheet. Bake at 400° for 6–8 minutes, or until brown.

Home Made with Love (Kentucky)

Pain Perdue

(Lost Bread or French Toast)

An old New Orleans favorite, this is a perfect use for less-than-fresh French bread.

1 (5-ounce) can evaporated
 milk
2 eggs, well beaten
½ cup sugar

½ teaspoon vanilla
5 slices French bread
1 cup oil or butter
Powdered sugar

Mix together evaporated milk, eggs, sugar, and vanilla; dip each slice of bread into this mixture, coating well. Drain off excess batter, and fry in hot oil at 375° until brown; turn and brown other side. Drain on paper towels, and sprinkle with powdered sugar. Serves 6.

Editor's Extra: I like to serve with sautéed sliced bananas on top.—*Barbara*

Cajun Cuisine (Louisiana)

Bobbi's Apple Pancakes

"I use it for recruits," says Bobbi Olson, wife of Lute Olson, former University of Arizona basketball coach. "They love it, and want their mothers to have the recipe."

CINNAMON SYRUP:
2 cups light corn syrup
4 cups sugar
1 cup water

1 tablespoon cinnamon
2 cups evaporated milk

In medium-size pot, combine all ingredients, except milk, and bring to a full boil. Cook for 2 minutes, stirring constantly. Let cool a full 5 minutes. Add milk, and serve warm with pancakes.

BATTER:
2 medium-size green apples,
 peeled, cored, and chopped
2 eggs
2 tablespoons sugar

2 tablespoons butter, softened
2 cups evaporated milk
2 cups Bisquick

While syrup is cooling, mix ingredients in a large bowl. Spoon onto greased pancake grill or frying pan, and cook over medium-high heat. Serves 4.

The Arizona Celebrity Cookbook (Arizona)

Morning Mix-Up

A little something extra for a great send-off.

2 cups frozen hash browns	**6 eggs**
1 cup chopped ham	**Salt and pepper to taste**
½ cup chopped onion	**1 cup shredded Cheddar cheese**
2 tablespoons oil	**Minced fresh chives**

Mix hash browns, ham, onion, and oil in large saucepan. Then cook on medium high for 10 minutes or more, till softened, stirring occasionally. Beat eggs, salt, and pepper. Add to mixture. Stir occasionally. Remove from heat, and gently stir in cheese. Sprinkle with chives. Serves 4–6.

Editor's Extra: Using frozen chopped onions and packaged diced ham makes this a snap of a tasty breakfast.

Costco Wholesale Employee Association Cookbook (Washington)

Breakfast Casserole Muffins

A hearty start . . . a great breakfast on the run.

1 pound bulk sausage, browned and drained	**2 cups half-and-half**
	½ teaspoon salt
6 eggs	**¼ teaspoon pepper**
1 cup Bisquick	**2 cups grated Cheddar cheese**

Place drained sausage evenly in muffin tins sprayed with cooking spray. Mix eggs, Bisquick, half-and-half, salt, and pepper. Pour evenly over the sausage. Top with grated cheese. Bake for 25 minutes in a 350° oven. Makes 24 muffins. They freeze well.

Treasured Recipes (Alabama)

I have many memories of waking up to eat breakfast that my mother carefully prepared for us and her saying, "What do y'all want for lunch," and as we're eating lunch, "What do y'all want for dinner?" It's always about the next meal.

—Lisa Loeb

Early Morning Quiche

Good late at night, too . . . and any time inbetween.

1 unbaked pastry shell	4 eggs, beaten
12 strips crisp bacon, crumbled	2 cups whipping cream
½ cup grated Monterey Jack cheese	¾ teaspoon salt
	¼ teaspoon sugar
½ cup grated Cheddar cheese	⅛ teaspoon cayenne pepper
⅓ cup chopped onion	

Line pastry shell with double thickness of foil. Bake at 450° for 5 minutes. Remove foil, and bake another 5 minutes. Remove from oven. Reduce heat to 425°. Sprinkle bacon, cheeses, and onion over crust. Beat eggs, cream, salt, sugar, and cayenne. Pour into crust. Bake for 15 minutes. Reduce heat to 300°, and bake 30 minutes longer or until knife inserted into center comes out clean. Serves 6–8.

Upper Kenai River Inn Breakfast Cookbook (Alaska)

Hash Brown Quiche

This spunky quiche served along with some fresh fruit is as good as it gets.

3 cups frozen hash browns, thawed, and pressed between paper towels	4 ounces shredded Swiss cheese
	6 ounces diced ham
	Salt to taste
⅓ cup melted margarine	2 eggs
4 ounces hot pepper cheese	½ cup whipping cream

Press well-dried hash browns on bottom and up sides of a 9-inch pie plate. Drizzle with melted margarine. Bake 10 minutes at 400°.

Process remaining ingredients in food processor. Pour over hash brown crust. Bake 35–45 minutes at 350° or until knife comes out clean. Let stand 10 minutes before serving. Can be served hot, cold, or at room temperature for breakfast, lunch, or as an appetizer. Serves 6–8.

If It Tastes Good, Who Cares? II (Great Plains)

Brunch Frittata

Quick, easy, and perfect for a relaxing time with the family.

1 tablespoon butter
1½–2 cups hash brown
   potatoes
8 slices bacon, cooked and
   crumbled, or ½ cup
   cubed ham

8–10 eggs
¾ cup cream of mushroom
   or celery soup (optional)
1½ cups shredded Cheddar
   cheese

Melt butter in a 10-inch skillet over moderate heat. Add hash browns, and partially cook. Top with bacon or ham. Beat eggs, and pour over ingredients in skillet. Cover pan, and turn heat to low. Cook 10–12 minutes, until eggs are set. Top with cream soup, if desired, and add Cheddar cheese the last few minutes of cooking. Cut into wedges, and serve. Serves 8.

Montezuma Amish Mennonite Cookbook II (Georgia)

Southwestern Eggs

Try this one time, and your family will be hooked!

10 eggs
1 stick margarine, melted
½ cup all-purpose flour
1 teaspoon baking powder
2 (4-ounce) cans chopped
   green chiles, drained

2 cups cottage cheese
1 teaspoon salt
Hot pepper sauce to taste
1 pound Monterey Jack
   cheese, shredded
Salsa

Preheat oven to 350°. Beat eggs well, then add remaining ingredients, except shredded cheese; fold in cheese. Spray a 9x13-inch dish with cooking spray. Bake 45 minutes or longer, until knife comes out firm. Can bake a day ahead, then reheat. Serve with salsa.

Sing for Your Supper (North Carolina)

Morning Pizza

Excellent recipe. It's a morning party!

¼ cup milk
5 eggs with a pinch of salt
1 package pizza crust mix
1 pound ground sausage,
  cooked and drained
2 cups frozen hash browns

¼ cup grated Parmesan cheese
1½ cups shredded cheese
  (a variety, if desired)
Chopped mushrooms, bell
  peppers, etc. (optional)
Picante sauce

Mix milk with slightly salted eggs, and scramble in skillet. Prepare pizza dough as directed on package, and pat into a 13-inch greased pizza pan. Spread crumbled sausage on dough. Cover with hash browns, Parmesan cheese, scrambled eggs, and shredded cheese, in that order. Add mushrooms and peppers, if desired. Bake at 375° for 25–30 minutes. Serve with picante sauce. Serves 8.

Just Inn Time for Breakfast (Michigan)

Breakfast Pizza

A hearty high-note recipe the whole family will enjoy.

1 (8-ounce) tube refrigerated
  crescent rolls
1 pound bulk pork sausage,
  hot or mild
1 cup frozen shredded hash
  brown potatoes, thawed

1 (4-ounce) package shredded
  Cheddar cheese
3 eggs
¼ cup milk
¼ teaspoon pepper
¼ cup grated Parmesan cheese

Unroll crescent dough, and place on greased 12-inch pizza pan; press seams together and press up sides of pan to form a crust. In a skillet, brown sausage over medium heat; drain, and cool slightly. Sprinkle sausage, hash browns, and Cheddar cheese over crust.

  In a bowl, beat eggs, milk, and pepper; pour over pizza. Sprinkle with Parmesan cheese. Bake at 375° for 28–30 minutes or until golden brown. Let stand 10 minutes before cutting. Serves 6–8.

Favorite Recipes from First Church of God (Ohio)

Morning Pizza

Banana Smoothie

When my kids were young, they voted me "Number 1 Mom" at a family reunion because I let them have shakes for breakfast. See what fresh juices or fruits are available at the grocery store or farmers' market, and have fun experimenting with different flavors.

1 small ripe banana, cut into chunks
½ cup fresh orange juice
½ cup canned unsweetened pineapple juice
½ cup plain yogurt
1 tablespoon sugar or honey to taste
Protein powder to taste (optional)
½ cup small or coarsely crushed ice cubes

In a blender, combine banana, orange juice, pineapple juice, yogurt, sugar, protein powder, and ice. Mix at high speed until smooth. Pour into 2 tall, frosty glasses.

Note: If crushing ice cubes is a problem for your blender, eliminate ice cubes, and freeze fruit and yogurt.

Editor's Extra: Smoothies are today's biggest aid to eating healthier easier. With a good blender, you can incorporate various fruits, veggies, yogurt, protein powder, local honey . . . and any number of things your family might otherwise not choose to eat. Adding chocolate, cherry juice, or orange juice makes it even tastier.

Summertime Treats (Oregon)

To put the world right in order, we must first put the nation in order; to put the nation in order, we must first put the family in order; to put the family in order, we must first cultivate our personal life; we must first set our hearts right.
—Confucius

Salads

Apple Cranberry Salad

A very merry toss-up.

1 bag mixed field greens
2 (3-ounce) packages goat
  cheese, crumbled
1 small bag (2 handfuls) dried
  cranberries

5 ounces pine nuts, toasted
1 large apple, chopped
½ red onion, chopped

Toss greens well. Add remaining ingredients, and toss.

DRESSING:
½ cup apple cider vinegar
¼ cup olive oil
½ cup sugar

½ teaspoon salt
½ teaspoon dry mustard

Whisk together all ingredients. Pour into a container with lid, and shake. Slowly pour ½ Dressing over salad. You will not need all of the Dressing. The recipe makes enough Dressing for 2 salads.

Editor's Extra: Feta cheese is equally good in this delicious salad.

Bountiful Blessings (Virginia)

Bacon-Egg-Spinach Salad

This is just plain good!

½ cup oil
¼ cup sugar
2 tablespoons vinegar
1 teaspoon finely grated onion
½ teaspoon salt
¼ teaspoon dry mustard

1 pound fresh spinach
6 slices crisp bacon, crumbled
5 hard-cooked eggs, chopped
1 hard-cooked egg, sliced for
  garnish

Combine oil, sugar, vinegar, onion, salt, and mustard; set aside. Wash spinach, drain on paper towels, and tear into bite-size pieces. Place in large salad bowl. Add bacon and chopped eggs. Pour dressing over spinach, toss, and let stand ½ hour. Garnish with sliced egg. Serves 8.

The Fine Art of Dining (Virginia)

Caesar Salad

The real deal. Superb.

2 large garlic cloves, peeled
  and crushed
½ teaspoon salt
¼ teaspoon black pepper
⅓ cup freshly squeezed lemon
  juice (or more to taste)
⅔ cup olive oil
2 teaspoons Worcestershire,
  or 1 anchovy, mashed, or
  ¼ teaspoon anchovy paste

Pinch of sugar
8 cups loosely packed romaine
  lettuce leaves, torn into
  bite-size pieces
⅓ cup grated Parmesan cheese
1–2 cups croutons (depending
  on how many you like
  in your salad)

In a small bowl, blend together garlic, salt, and pepper. Whisk in lemon juice. Slowly add oil. Add Worcestershire or anchovy and a pinch of sugar. Whisk until blended well. In a large bowl, gently toss together lettuce and dressing, adding Parmesan cheese and croutons. Serves 4.

Gourmet: The Quick and Easy Way (Oklahoma)

Better-Than-"Store-Bought" Croutons

So good they'll make kids be more inclined to eat the salad around them.

Butter
Bread slices
Parmesan cheese

Seasoned salt
Italian seasoning

Butter bread slices. Sprinkle Parmesan cheese over bread, then seasoned salt, then Italian seasoning. Freeze slightly. (This makes cutting easier.) Cut into cubes. Preheat oven to 350°. Turn oven off. Put bread cubes on a baking pan, 1 layer thick; put in oven; allow to remain overnight. Place in airtight container. Keeps indefinitely. So good on top of a tossed salad, floating on soup, or crushed into crumbs for a special topping.

High Cotton Cookin' (Arkansas)

Picnic Pasta Salad

A versatile salad that goes well with most anything. Don't wait for a picnic.

8 ounces uncooked macaroni,
  any style
8 ounces Italian dressing
1 tablespoon Dijon mustard
¼ teaspoon black pepper
2 cups assorted frozen vegetables,
  thawed and drained

1 medium red or green bell
  pepper, or mixture, chopped
½ cup sliced ripe olives
2 tablespoons chopped fresh
  parsley

Cook macaroni according to package directions; drain, and rinse with cold water until completely cool. Blend Italian dressing, mustard, and pepper in large bowl; stir in vegetables, bell pepper, olives, and parsley. Add macaroni; toss well. Cover; chill at least 2 hours.

Four Seasons Cookbook (Michigan)

Taco Salad

A meal in itself, this fits in nicely with weekend comings and goings.

1 pound ground beef, browned
1 (15-ounce) can kidney beans
  (optional)
4 cups chopped lettuce
1 small cucumber, sliced
1 green bell pepper, chopped
½ cup chopped green onions

2 tomatoes, chopped
½ cup chopped olives (optional)
2 cups crushed tortilla chips
½ cup (or more) grated Cheddar
  cheese
Favorite salad dressing
Taco sauce

Brown ground beef; drain. Drain beans, if using, and add to ground beef, just to heat. In large bowl, combine lettuce, cucumber, green pepper, onions, tomatoes, olives, if desired, and chips. Add meat and beans; toss. Sprinkle with cheese. Serve with your favorite salad dressing and as much taco sauce as you dare. Refrigerate if not serving right away. Serves 6.

Editor's Extra: I like to transfer this to a pretty 9x13-inch baking dish before sprinkling with cheese.

Kinder Bakker (Michigan)

Picnic Pasta Salad

Layered Salad Supreme

A salad with a whole-lotta goodness goin' on . . . for a whole lotta people.

DRESSING:

3 cups mayonnaise
1 cup sour cream

2 teaspoons seasoned salt
1 teaspoon garlic powder

Combine mayonnaise, sour cream, seasoned salt, and garlic powder; set aside.

SALAD:

2 quarts chopped lettuce
3 cups chopped green bell
  peppers
1¼ quarts shredded carrots
1¼ quarts sliced cauliflower
1 quart chopped cucumbers
1 quart sliced celery
3 cups sliced radishes

3½ cups chopped zucchini
2⅔ cups sliced red onions
1 pound bacon, cooked and
  chopped
6 hard-cooked eggs, chopped
1 cup parsley, minced
6 cherry tomatoes

In 2-gallon punch bowl, layer and pack the lettuce, green peppers, carrots, cauliflower, 2 cups Dressing, cucumbers, celery, radishes, zucchini, onions, and remaining 2 cups Dressing. Cover; refrigerate a few hours.

At serving time, sprinkle bacon around edge, and fill center with chopped eggs. Garnish with parsley and tomatoes. Makes 2 gallons.

Editor's Extra: This makes enough for a large family gathering. Easy to halve or quarter.

Koinonia Cooking (Tennessee)

The colors of a fresh garden salad are so extraordinary, no painter's pallet can duplicate nature's artistry.
—Dr. SunWolf

Waldorf Coleslaw

Enormously tasty!

½ cup thinly sliced celery
½ cup thinly sliced sweet onion
½ cup dried sweetened
   cranberries
½ Braeburn apple, unpeeled,
   thinly sliced
½ cup chopped walnuts

Sea salt to taste
Freshly ground black pepper
   to taste
½ cup light slaw dressing*
1 (16-ounce) package angel hair
   cabbage slaw

Combine all ingredients, except cabbage, and toss till thoroughly coated. Add cabbage, and toss till well coated. Refrigerate till ready to serve. May be prepared in the morning for an evening meal. Serves 4–6.

*Note: Marzetti's dressing is recommended.

Heart of the Harbor (Virginia)

Broccoli and Raisin Salad

Very good, very crunchy, with a sweet, pungent flavor.

2 bunches broccoli
⅓ cup sugar
⅔ cup raisins
½ cup chopped onion

2 tablespoons vinegar
1 cup mayonnaise
4 bacon slices, cooked and
   crumbled

Blanch broccoli for 2 minutes, if you wish. Cut off florets, and cut into serving pieces; discard stems. Freshen florets in ice water for 5 minutes; drain, and dry. Place florets in a salad bowl. Mix together sugar, raisins, onion, vinegar, and mayonnaise. Pour dressing over broccoli, and toss lightly. (Can be prepared an hour or so in advance; cover and refrigerate.) Just before serving, add crumbled bacon on top. Serves 8–10.

Editor's Extra: Blanch means to plunge briefly in hot water. This helps raw broccoli to be friendlier with your teeth. But some people prefer it raw and crunchy.

The Lymes' Heritage Cookbook (New England)

Curried Chicken Salad in Tomato Petals

A superb chicken salad for sandwiches, or to pile on lettuce, or simply serve on a thick tomato slice if you want it a bit less fussy. Yum!

2 cups cooked, diced chicken
1 apple, pared and diced
½ cup diced celery
2 teaspoons grated onion
½ cup halved seedless grapes
⅓ cup toasted, slivered
   almonds

2 teaspoons curry powder
1 cup mayonnaise
1 teaspoon salt
Dash of pepper
6 tomatoes

Combine chicken, apple, celery, onion, grapes, and almonds. Blend curry powder with mayonnaise and seasonings; stir into chicken mixture. Chill. Cut tomatoes in sixths, almost but not all the way through, to form petals. Fill with chicken salad. Serves 6.

Favorite Island Cookery Book II (Hawaii)

Dried Cherry Chicken Salad

A delightfully tart-ish take on a feeds-a-lot favorite.

1 cup dried tart red cherries
4 chicken breast halves, cooked,
   torn into large pieces
3 stalks celery, coarsely chopped
2 Granny Smith apples,
   coarsely chopped

1 cup coarsely chopped pecans
1¼ cups mayonnaise
½ cup chopped parsley
1 tablespoon raspberry vinegar
Salt and pepper to taste
Red leaf lettuce

Mix cherries, chicken, celery, apples, and pecans in a large bowl. Combine mayonnaise, parsley, and raspberry vinegar in a bowl; mix well. Add to chicken mixture, and toss lightly to coat well. Season with salt and pepper. Chill 2 hours or longer. Serve on a bed of red leaf lettuce. Garnish with additional cherries, if desired. Serves 6 or more.

Editor's Extra: Dried cranberries are a good sub for dried cherries.

The Dexter Cider Mill Apple Cookbook (Michigan)

Shrimp Salad

A lovely shrimp salad stretched to feed a few more by adding a few potatoes.

SALAD:

1 pound well-seasoned boiled shrimp, peeled

3 small red potatoes, peeled, boiled in shrimp water

2 hard-boiled eggs, peeled and chopped

2 tablespoons chopped onion

¼ cup chopped celery

Save the shrimp water to boil potatoes. If using crab boil bag to season shrimp, remove before boiling potatoes. Cool and cube potatoes. Mix all ingredients, and add Dressing. Chill until ready to serve. Serve on crisp lettuce leaves. Serves 4.

DRESSING:

¼ cup (heaping) mayonnaise

3 teaspoons Durkee's dressing (more according to taste)

½ teaspoon salt

¼ teaspoon black pepper

Sprinkling of red pepper

Sprinkling of dill weed

Combine ingredients. Mix. Check seasonings for taste.

Turnip Greens in the Bathtub (Louisiana)

Family is often born of blood, but it doesn't depend on blood. Nor is it exclusive of friendship. Family members can be your best friends, you know. And best friends, whether or not they are related to you, can be your family.

—Trenton Lee Steward,
The Mysterious Benedict Society

Heavenly Orange Fluff

A light and lovely favorite. Just as satisfying as a dessert the next day.

2 (3-ounce) packages orange
  Jell-O
2½ cups boiling water
1 (15-ounce) can crushed
  pineapple, undrained
½ (12-ounce) can frozen orange
  juice concentrate, thawed

2 (11-ounce) cans mandarin
  oranges, drained
1 (3¾-ounce) package instant
  vanilla pudding mix
1 cup cold milk
1 cup whipping cream, whipped

Dissolve Jell-O in boiling water; add undrained pineapple and orange juice concentrate. Chill until partially set, about 40 minutes. Fold in oranges; pour into 9x13-inch baking dish. Chill until firm.

Beat pudding and milk with rotary beater until smooth. Fold in whipped cream; spread over gelatin. Chill. Serves 12–15.

Calvary's Cuisine (California)

If the family were a fruit, it would be an orange, a circle of sections, held together but separable—each segment distinct.
    —Letty Cottin Pogrebin

Heavenly Orange Fluff

Six Cup Salad

1 cup sour cream
1 cup shredded coconut
1 cup miniature marshmallows
1 cup mandarin oranges,
   drained

1 cup crushed pineapple, drained
1 cup chopped pecans
12 maraschino cherries (halved)

Combine all ingredients, except cherries, in a 2-quart bowl. Refrigerate 24 hours. Garnish with cherries.

Christ Reformed Church Historical Cookbook (West Virginia)

Make-Ahead Fruit Salad

The marshmallow dressing caresses the fruit.

1 (15-ounce) can pineapple
   chunks
1 (15-ounce) can fruit cocktail
1 (11-ounce) can mandarin
   oranges
½ pound marshmallows

¼ cup fresh lemon juice
1 cup flaked coconut
½ cup chopped nuts (almonds,
   walnuts, or pecans)
1 cup fresh or frozen berries
   (strawberries or raspberries)

Drain and reserve juice from pineapple, fruit cocktail, and mandarin oranges. Set juice aside. Combine fruits in bowl.

Melt marshmallows in double boiler over gently boiling water until completely melted. Add 1 cup of fruit juice and ¼ cup lemon juice to melted marshmallows. Combine coconut, nuts, and berries, and add to fruit mixture. Fold marshmallow dressing into the combined mixture. Cover, and chill several hours or overnight. Serves 6–8.

Truly Montana Cookbook (Big Sky)

Call it a clan, call it a network, call it a tribe, call it a family: whatever you call it, whoever you are, you need one.
                    —Jane Howard

Vegetables & Sides

Twice Baked Potatoes

You can never serve these often enough. THE BEST!

6 medium baking potatoes
1 teaspoon salt
⅛ teaspoon pepper
¼ cup butter
½ cup sour cream

1 cup shredded Cheddar cheese
1–2 tablespoons chopped chives
2–4 tablespoons cooked,
   crumbled bacon

Bake potatoes at 400° for 45–60 minutes or until tender. Cut in halves lengthwise. Scoop potatoes out of shells into bowl, and mash. Add remaining ingredients, and beat until light and fluffy. Spoon back into shells. Sprinkle with additional cheese and bake, uncovered, 20–25 minutes until hot. Serves 6.

Editor's Extra: If stiff, beat in a little warm milk.

Victorian Sampler (Arkansas)

Creamy Sweet Hash Brown Casserole

A crowd-pleaser every time.

1 (22-ounce) package frozen
   hash browns, thawed
1 (10¾-ounce) can cream of
   chicken soup
1 (10¾-ounce) can cream of
   mushroom soup

1 (8-ounce) carton sour cream
10 ounces shredded Cheddar
   cheese
⅛ cup minced onion
1 stick butter
Salt and pepper to taste

Mix all ingredients, and pour into 9x13-inch baking dish or pan. Bake at 350° for 50 minutes. Sprinkle with Topping, and bake 10 minutes more. Serves 6–8.

TOPPING:
2 cups frosted flakes, crushed   ¼ stick butter, melted

Toss together.

Bethany's Best Bites (Alabama)

Crunch-Top Potatoes

Once they've tasted this, there's no need to call them twice when you serve this kid-friendly potato casserole.

⅓ cup butter or margarine
3–4 large baking potatoes, peeled, sliced
¾ cup crushed cornflakes

1½ cups shredded sharp Cheddar cheese
1½ teaspoons paprika
Salt, if desired

Melt butter in 8x8-inch pan at 375°. Toss potatoes around in the butter. Mix remaining ingredients; sprinkle over. Bake ½ hour or until done. Serves 4.

Tumm Yummies (Ohio)

Bacon-Cheese Mashed Potatoes

A recipe to write home about . . . or to text or tweet.

4 baking potatoes (russet), about 3 pounds, peeled, cut into 1-inch pieces
1¾ teaspoons salt, divided
½ cup heavy cream
4 tablespoons butter
¼ teaspoon ground black pepper

8 slices bacon, cooked crisp and crumbled
½ pound sharp Cheddar cheese, grated
¼ cup sour cream
¼ cup chopped fresh chives
Freshly ground black pepper

Place potatoes and 1 teaspoon salt in a heavy 4-quart saucepan, and cover with water by 1 inch. Bring to a boil. Reduce heat to a simmer, and cook until the potatoes are fork-tender, about 20 minutes. Drain. Add cream, butter, remaining ¾ teaspoon salt, and black pepper. Place the pan over medium-low heat, and mash with a potato masher to incorporate the ingredients, and achieve a light texture, 4–5 minutes. Add bacon, grated cheese, sour cream, and chopped chives, and stir until thoroughly combined. Season to taste. Serve immediately. Serves 6.

CASA Cooks (Nevada)

Pizza Potatoes

Really easy and really yummy.

1 (7½-ounce) package scalloped
  potatoes
1 (14½-ounce) can tomatoes
1½ cups water
¼ teaspoon crushed oregano
  leaves

1 (4-ounce) package sliced
  pepperoni
1 (4-ounce) package shredded
  mozzarella cheese

Heat oven to 400°. Empty potato slices and packet of seasoned sauce mix into ungreased 2-quart casserole. Heat tomatoes, water, and oregano to boiling; stir into potatoes. Arrange pepperoni on top, and sprinkle with cheese. Bake uncovered 30 minutes. Serves 4.

Note: May substitute ½ pound beef, browned and drained, for pepperoni; stir into potato mixture.

Recipe submitted by Cindy Shifflet Lee (Miss Virginia Farm Bureau 1978)
Country Treasures (Virginia)

Cheesy Fries

Pie pan fires! Easy, cheesy, good!

3 medium potatoes
3 tablespoons butter or
  margarine
¼ cup grated Parmesan cheese

½ teaspoon garlic powder
½ teaspoon seasoned salt
½ teaspoon paprika

Preheat oven to 375°. Scrub potatoes, leaving skins on. Cut each potato into 8 wedges. Melt butter or margarine in a large pie pan in oven. Dip wedges in melted butter, and arrange in a donut pattern in pan. Combine cheese and spices. Sprinkle evenly over potatoes. Bake 25–30 minutes until potatoes are just about tender.

Editor's Extra: The smaller the cut, the faster they bake.

Smyth County Extension Homemakers Cookbook (Virginia)

Sweet Potato Soufflé

If you want to "wow" your guests for the holidays, this recipe will do it!

TOPPING:

1 cup brown sugar
⅓ stick butter, melted
⅓ cup all-purpose flour
1 cup chopped pecans or walnuts

Mix Topping ingredients well; set aside.

3 cups mashed sweet potatoes
  (may use canned)
2 eggs
⅓ stick butter, melted
½ teaspoon salt
½ cup milk
1 cup sugar
1 teaspoon vanilla

Mix ingredients well; put in greased 7x10-inch baking dish, and sprinkle Topping over potatoes. Bake in 350° oven for 35 minutes. Serves 8–10. (All can be made ahead and frozen; thaw before baking.)

Fabulous Favorites (California)

Crispy Fried Carrots

Get ready to make these again and again . . . they are THAT good.

¾ cup cornmeal
¾ cup all-purpose flour
1 teaspoon onion powder
2½ tablespoons chopped fresh
  parsley
½ teaspoon salt
½ teaspoon ground black
  pepper
1 teaspoon Old Bay Seasoning
1 egg white
⅔ cup buttermilk
½ teaspoon hot sauce
4 large carrots, scraped and cut
  into thin strips
Vegetable oil

Combine cornmeal, flour, onion powder, chopped parsley, salt, pepper, and Old Bay Seasoning. Set aside. Beat egg white until foamy. Stir in buttermilk and hot sauce. Dip carrots into buttermilk mixture. Drain off excess, and dredge in cornmeal mixture. Pour oil to depth of 1 inch into a Dutch oven. Heat to 350°. Fry carrots 2 minutes or until lightly browned. Serve immediately. Serves 4–6.

Kay's Kitchen (Alaska)

Tomato Cheese Pie

This lovely dish is especially good in summer when tomatoes are in season. Add a salad for a light meal.

1 (7.5-ounce) tube buttermilk
 biscuits
2–3 large tomatoes, sliced
Salt and pepper to taste
Sweet basil to taste
1 small green bell pepper,
 sliced

1 large onion, sliced
1 cup sliced mushrooms
¼ cup olive oil
1½ cups mayonnaise (or less)
1 cup grated Cheddar, Monterey
 Jack, or mozzarella cheese

Line a greased deep 10-inch pie dish with biscuits, pressing edges together to form a crust. Place half of tomatoes on biscuits. Season with sprinkles of salt, pepper, and basil. Sauté green pepper, onion, and mushrooms in oil. Drain. Place on top of tomatoes. Add remaining tomatoes. Season again. Mix well mayonnaise and cheese, and spread over top. Bake at 350° for 40–45 minutes. Serves 6.

Editor's Extra: Add 2 egg whites to the mayo/cheese mixture if you want the topping to stand up higher and cut easier.

All in Good Taste I (Wisconsin)

Puffy Coated Onion Rings

Absolutely delicious. Your family will definitely ask for these again and again!

2 large onions
2 eggs, separated
1¼ cups buttermilk
1½ tablespoons oil

1¼ cups all-purpose flour
1 teaspoon salt
1¼ teaspoons baking powder

Peel onions, and slice ¼ inch thick. Separate into rings. Beat egg yolks. Add buttermilk, oil, and sifted dry ingredients. Beat egg whites until stiff. Fold into buttermilk mixture. Dip onion rings into batter. Fry, a few at a time, in deep fat (375°). Drain thoroughly on paper towels, and sprinkle with additional salt. Keep in warm oven. Serves 4.

Note: May be frozen. When ready to serve, place frozen onion rings on baking sheet, and heat at 450° for 5 minutes.

Onions Make the Meal Cookbook (Idaho)

Tomato Cheese Pie

Cauliflower and Cheese

A nice and easy vegetable to bring to the table.

½ head fresh cauliflower
2 cups water
½ teaspoon salt
4 tablespoons mayonnaise

1 teaspoon prepared mustard
½ cup grated or shredded
  Cheddar cheese

Preheat oven to 375°. Remove outer green leaves from cauliflower, and wash under running water. In saucepan over medium heat, bring water to a boil. Add salt and cauliflower, cover, reduce heat, and slowly boil for 15 minutes. Carefully remove cauliflower to a baking dish (use a flat spatula to keep it from breaking up). Combine mayonnaise, mustard, and cheese; spread over cauliflower. Bake for 10–15 minutes.

This makes a good dish for company, since you can prepare it in advance, waiting to bake until just before serving.

The Bachelor's Cookbook (Georgia)

Creamy Spinach

A wonderful side dish, this is quick and easy to prepare.

3 slices bacon, chopped
1 leek, cleaned and chopped
1 cup sliced baby Portobello
  mushrooms
3 tablespoons butter, divided

1 (6-ounce) bag baby spinach,
  washed
2–3 tablespoons heavy cream
⅓ cup grated Parmesan cheese

In a large skillet, sauté bacon, leek, and mushrooms in 1½ tablespoons butter until golden brown. Add remaining 1½ tablespoons butter and spinach; heat on low until wilted. Pour in cream; mix well. Add cheese, and stir until melted. Serve immediately. Serves 2.

Editor's Extra: Sub 2 chopped green onions or a tablespoon of any diced onion for leek. Perk it up with a few sprinkles of your favorite seasoning mix.

Gloriously Gluten-Free (Virginia)

Squash Casserole

A super delicious vegetable dish.

3 pounds yellow squash, sliced
5 tablespoons butter, divided
1 small onion, chopped
1 cup shredded sharp Cheddar
   cheese
2 large eggs, lightly beaten

¼ cup mayonnaise
2 teaspoons sugar
1 teaspoon salt
20 round buttery crackers,
   crushed

In large skillet, cook squash in boiling water to cover for 8–10 minutes, or just till tender. Drain well. Gently press between paper towels.

Melt 4 tablespoons butter in same skillet over medium-high heat; add onion, and sauté 5 minutes, till tender. Remove skillet from heat; stir in squash, cheese, eggs, mayonnaise, sugar, and salt. Spoon mixture into a lightly greased 7x11-inch baking dish. Melt remaining 1 tablespoon butter; stir together with crushed crackers; sprinkle evenly over top of casserole. Bake at 350° for 30–35 minutes, or till set.

Editor's Extra: Toss some chopped green or red bell pepper into sauté with the onion. Pretty and tasty.

The Sun and the Rain & the Appleseed (Virginia)

Your family and your love must be cultivated like a garden. Time, effort, and imagination must be summoned constantly to keep any relationship flourishing and growing.

—Jim Rohn

*Green Beans with
Honey-Roasted Pecans*

Green Beans with Honey-Roasted Pecans

Fit for a king . . . and all his kingdom.

HONEY-ROASTED PECANS:

¾ **cup pecan halves**	1 **tablespoon honey**

Preheat oven to 400°. Toss pecans with honey in a bowl. Spread honey-coated pecans in a single layer on an oiled baking sheet. Roast 8 minutes, stirring occasionally. Remove pecans to a sheet of wax paper or foil to cool.

GREEN BEANS:

1¼ **pounds fresh green beans, trimmed**	½ **cup chicken stock**
¼ **cup julienned red bell pepper**	1 **teaspoon peanut oil**
	Salt and pepper to taste

Combine beans, bell pepper, stock, peanut oil, salt, and pepper in a saucepan. Cook, covered, over high heat 3 minutes; remove cover. Cook over medium heat until stock evaporates and beans are tender-crisp, stirring occasionally. Spoon beans into a serving bowl. Top with Honey-Roasted Pecans. Serves 6.

Editor's Extra: Try adding roasted red bell pepper as a topping with the pecans.

Provisions & Politics (Tennessee)

Broccoli Supreme

Those little green trees never tasted better.

4 **cups cut broccoli buds and stems, cooked**	¾ **cup sour cream**
1 **(10¾-ounce) can cream of mushroom soup**	1 **cup sliced celery**
	½ **teaspoon pepper**
1 **(2-ounce) jar sliced pimentos**	1 **teaspoon salt**
	½ **cup grated Cheddar cheese**

Combine all ingredients, except cheese. Place in large buttered casserole dish. Top with cheese. Bake in a 350° oven for 20–25 minutes. Serves 6.

Dinner Bell (Pennsylvania)

Corn Pudding Tennessee Style

This finds its way to the Thanksgiving table by request.

2 cups corn, fresh or canned,
   drained
4 tablespoons all-purpose flour
2 level teaspoons sugar

1 level teaspoon salt
2 eggs, well beaten
2 tablespoons butter, melted
2 cups milk

Mix corn, flour, sugar, and salt. Combine well-beaten eggs, melted butter, and milk. Stir into corn mixture. Pour into greased 1½- or 2-quart baking dish. Bake at 350° for 1 hour. Stir from bottom 2–3 times during first 30 minutes of baking. Serves 6.

Tennessee Homecoming: Famous Parties, People & Places (Tennessee)

Corn Casserole

Who doesn't love corn casserole? Especially when it's this good.

1 (17-ounce) can whole-kernel
   corn, drained
1 (17-ounce) can cream-style
   corn
1 box Jiffy Corn Muffin Mix
1 stick butter or margarine

1 medium to large onion,
   chopped
1 green bell pepper, chopped
1 (8-ounce) carton sour cream
2 cups grated sharp Cheddar
   cheese

Combine corns and dry Jiffy. In medium saucepan, melt butter, and sauté onion and pepper. Place corn mixture in greased 9x13-inch baking pan. Spoon onion mixture over corn. Spoon sour cream over onion mixture. Top with cheese. Bake at 350° for 30 minutes.

Note: Better if made the night before; refrigerate before baking, and bake as directed. Can be frozen; thaw before baking.

Gibson/Goree Family Favorites (Alabama)

To me, the kitchen is a place of adventure and entirely fun, not drudgery. I can't think of anything better to do with family and friends than to be together to create something.

—Ted Allen

Cotton Eyed Joe's Baked Beans

Cotton Eyed Joe's is a serious barbecue stop on the south edge of Claremore, Oklahoma, just across the railroad track from Route 66.

2 (16-ounce) cans pork and
   beans
⅛ teaspoon salt
3½ tablespoons brown sugar
2 tablespoons Worcestershire

¼ cup barbecue sauce
1 teaspoon powdered mustard
3 drops liquid smoke
1 teaspoon powdered onion

Combine all ingredients in a large casserole dish, and bake at 300° for one hour. Serves 10.

The Route 66 Cookbook (Oklahoma)

Cajun Red Beans and Rice

Firs', Cher, you take one-two pound dem red bean an' put dem in a big pot, dere. Den you wash dem bean real good an' watch out fo' dem little rock an' chuck dirt. Wen dem bean real good clean, fill up wit' planty water, fo'-five quart. Trow in nice ham bone wit planty meat lef' on, or one-two pound ham chuck. Don' fo'get to remember two-free onion, fo'-five toe garlic, an' planty salt an' pepper. Now boil dat all down til dem bean planty soft an' dat gravy planty thick. Serve dem over steam rice wit' Tabasco Sauce, Cher. An' bon appétit!

TRANSLATION:
2 pounds dried red beans
4–5 quarts water
1 meaty ham bone, or 1½
   pounds ham chunks
2 large onions, chopped

4 garlic cloves, minced
1 bay leaf (optional)
Salt and pepper to taste
Cooked rice
Tabasco to taste

Rinse beans. Remove any foreign matter, such as stems, etc. Place in a large (4- to 6-quart) saucepan or Dutch oven. Add water, ham, onions, garlic, and seasonings. Simmer slowly for about 3 hours, until beans are soft and gravy is thick. Serve over cooked rice with Tabasco Sauce. Serves 10.

'Tiger Bait' Recipes (Louisiana)

Sister Marla's Dirty Rice

Don't let the name scare you . . . this recipe gets a thumbs up from the entire family.

1 cup uncooked rice	1 tablespoon Worcestershire
⅓ cup chopped green onions	½ tablespoon liquid smoke
¼ cup diced red bell pepper	¾ teaspoon cumin
2 tablespoons bacon drippings	Salt and pepper to taste
(or cooking spray or butter)	2 cups beef broth

Sauté rice, onion, and bell pepper in bacon drippings until golden. Stir in remaining ingredients, and bring to a boil. Cover tightly, and reduce heat. Cook slowly for 20 minutes without lifting lid. Serves 4–6.

First Baptist Favorites (Arizona)

Stuffed Green Peppers

An easy microwave rendition of a summertime classic.

1 pound lean ground beef	½ teaspoon cayenne pepper
⅔ cup Italian bread crumbs	¼ cup chopped green bell pepper
1 egg	4 medium green bell peppers,
1 (8-ounce) can tomato sauce,	washed and halved
divided	1 (15½-ounce) jar Ragu
2 tablespoons water	spaghetti sauce
¾ teaspoon salt	

In medium mixing bowl, mix beef, bread crumbs, egg, ½ can tomato sauce, water, salt, cayenne pepper, and chopped bell pepper. Fill bell pepper halves with beef mixture. Place in a 7x11-inch oblong casserole dish.

Pour remaining ½ can tomato sauce and Ragu sauce over filled peppers. Cover with plastic wrap. Microwave on 70% power for 25 minutes. Let stand 10 minutes. Serves 8.

Southern Spice à la Microwave (Louisiana)

Crockpot Dressing

Free up the oven for the turkey. You won't believe how good this is!

1 pan (or skillet) cornbread,
  cut up
4 slices white bread, cut up
1 onion, chopped
3 eggs, beaten
1 stick butter or margarine,
  melted
1 (10¾-ounce) can cream of
  celery soup

1 tablespoon sage
1 teaspoon black pepper
1½ teaspoons salt, or to taste
1 teaspoon poultry seasoning
3–4 cups chicken broth or stock
1 (2- to 3-pound) fryer, cooked
  and deboned (optional)

Mix ingredients with broth until medium-thin consistency. Stir in chicken, if desired. Pour into crockpot. Cook on HIGH for 2 hours, stirring several times. Turn on LOW; continue to cook 4–6 hours or until the dressing is the consistency you like. Easily serves 10–12.

Look Who Came to Dinner (Mississippi)

Broccoli Dressing

Take this dish to the next family gathering, and you'll be getting recipe requests all evening!

1 bunch broccoli, chopped,
  cooked, drained
2 cups dry stuffing mix
1 medium onion, chopped
2 stalks celery, chopped
1 (10¾-ounce) can cream of
  mushroom soup

2 egg whites, beaten
½ cup mayonnaise
1 teaspoon sage
½ cup chicken broth
3 tablespoons butter or
  margarine, melted

Preheat oven to 325°. Mix all ingredients, except melted butter. Put in greased 2-quart casserole dish, and pour melted butter on top. Bake 30–35 minutes.

Let Me Serve You (South Carolina)

Deluxe Macaroni and Cheese

Creamy and cheesy. The ultimate comfort food.

2 cups small-curd cottage
  cheese
1 cup sour cream
1 egg, lightly beaten
¼ teaspoon salt

Garlic salt and pepper to taste
2 cups shredded sharp Cheddar
  cheese
½ (7-ounce) package elbow
  macaroni, cooked, drained

In large bowl, combine cottage cheese, sour cream, egg, salt, garlic salt, and pepper. Add Cheddar cheese; mix well. Add cooked macaroni, and stir until coated. Transfer to a greased 2½-quart baking dish. Bake, uncovered, at 350° for 25–30 minutes, or until heated through. Serves 6–8.

Red Flannel Town Recipes (Michigan)

Cheese Grits Casserole

A nice alternative to pasta, rice, or potatoes. Superb!

4 cups water
1 teaspoon salt
1 cup quick grits
½ stick butter

2 cups shredded sharp Cheddar
  cheese
3 eggs, well beaten

Boil water and salt. Add grits, and stir constantly until mixed. Cook 3–5 minutes. Add butter, cheese, and eggs; mix well. Pour into greased 2-quart baking dish. Bake at 350° for 30–40 minutes.

Editor's Extra: Try pimento cheese as a substitute for Cheddar. Delicious!

From Our Home to Yours (North Carolina)

Bringing up family should be an adventure, not an anxious discipline in which everybody is constantly graded for performance.
—Milton R. Saperstein

Soups & Sandwiches

Loaded Potato Soup

⅔ cup butter or margarine
⅔ cup all-purpose flour
7 cups milk
4 baking potatoes, baked, cooled, peeled, and cubed (about 4 cups)
4 green onions, sliced

1 cup (8 ounces) sour cream
1¼ cups shredded Cheddar cheese
12 bacon strips, cooked and crumbled
¾ teaspoon salt
½ teaspoon pepper

In a large kettle or Dutch oven, melt butter. Whisk in flour. Heat and stir until smooth. Gradually add milk, stirring constantly until thickened. Add potatoes and onions. Bring to a boil, stirring constantly. Reduce heat. Simmer 10 minutes. Add remaining ingredients. Stir until cheese is melted. Serve immediately. Garnish each serving with additional bacon, cheese, and green onion, if desired. Serves 8.

Editor's Extra: Multitask by baking extra potatoes for supper the night before, or bake along with something else. Cool, refrigerate, then peel and cut next day.

Sharing Our Best–Franklin (Tennessee)

Broccoli-Cauliflower-Cheese Soup

No problem getting your family to eat broccoli and cauliflower when you serve this tasty soup.

3 chicken bouillon cubes
3 cups water
½ cup diced celery
½ cup diced carrots
¼ cup diced onion
1 cup chopped broccoli

1 cup chopped cauliflower
6 cups milk
½ cup butter, melted
2 tablespoons flour
½ pound Velveeta cheese, cubed

Dissolve bouillon cubes in water in a large pot. Add vegetables, and cook until tender. Add milk. Combine melted butter and flour until smooth, add to soup mixture, and stir. Simmer. Add cheese; stir until cheese is melted.

Editor's Extra: Granulated bouillon dissolves so much easier than cubes. Sub 3 teaspoons for the cubes, or 3 cups canned broth for cubes and water.

Recipes from the Heart (Nevada)

Vegetable Cheddar Chowder

A make-ahead, sure-to-please cheesy chowder.

½ cup chopped onion
1 clove garlic, pressed
1 cup sliced celery
¾ cup sliced carrots
1 cup peeled, cubed potatoes
3½ cups chicken broth
1 (15-ounce) can corn, drained
¼ cup butter

¼ cup all-purpose flour
2 cups milk
1 tablespoon mustard
¼ teaspoon white pepper
⅛ teaspoon paprika
2 tablespoons diced pimento
2 cups shredded Cheddar cheese

In Dutch oven, combine onion, garlic, celery, carrots, potatoes, and chicken broth. Bring to a boil; cover, and reduce heat. Simmer 15–20 minutes. Stir in corn, and remove from heat.

In a saucepan, melt butter over low heat. Add flour, and stir till smooth. Cook 1 minute. Gradually add milk. Cook over medium heat, stirring constantly, till thick and bubbly. Stir in remaining ingredients. Cook till cheese melts. Gradually add cheese mixture to vegetables. Cook over medium heat till chowder is thoroughly heated. Makes 2 quarts and serves 6–8. Best when made a day ahead.

Editor's Extra: To bring out the flavor even more, add a teaspoon of your favorite all-in-one seasoning . . . Old Bay, Tony's, Cavender's, etc. Stretch it by adding a can of creamed corn.

Stir Crazy! (South Carolina)

To the outside world, we all grow old. But not to brothers and sisters. We know each other as we always were. We know each other's hearts. We share private family jokes. We remember family feuds and secrets, family griefs and joys. We live outside the touch of time.
—Clara Ortega

Corn Soup

This soup, with its south-of-the-border flavors, is popular throughout the Southwest. Served with tostadas and a green salad, it makes a complete meal.

3½ cups corn kernels,
   preferably fresh
1 cup chicken stock
2 tablespoons butter
2 cups milk
1 clove garlic, minced
1 teaspoon oregano

Salt and pepper to taste
2 tablespoons canned diced
   green chiles, drained
1 cup peeled, seeded, chopped
   tomatoes
1 cup cubed Monterey Jack
   cheese

Purée corn and stock in a blender or food processor. Place purée in a saucepan with butter. Stir and simmer 5 minutes. Add milk, garlic, oregano, salt, and pepper, and bring to a boil. Reduce heat, add chiles, and simmer 5 minutes. Divide tomatoes among 4 soup bowls. Remove soup from heat, and add cheese. Stir until just melted. Ladle over tomatoes in bowls. Serves 4.

A Little Southwest Cookbook (New Mexico)

Pumpkin Soup

We wish we had a dollar for every time we've handed out this recipe!

2 pounds fresh pumpkin
3 cups scalded coffee cream
   or milk
1 tablespoon butter

2 teaspoons maple syrup
1 teaspoon salt
⅛ teaspoon nutmeg

Steam the fresh pumpkin, then mash. Stir into the milk, then add the remaining ingredients. Heat, but do not boil, and serve immediately. Serves 6–8.

Note: May substitute 3 cups canned pumpkin for fresh.

The Country Innkeepers' Cookbook (New England)

Bean Soup with Ham Bone

Good sturdy soup is good for what ails you.

1 pound dried navy or pinto
  beans
5½ cups water
1 ham bone with some meat
½ cup chopped onion
½ cup chopped celery
½ cup chopped carrot
1½ teaspoons salt

¼ teaspoon black pepper
¼ teaspoon oregano or other
  seasoning
Several drops liquid smoke
  (optional)
2 chicken bouillon cubes,
  crushed, or 2 teaspoons
  granules

Combine beans and water in large stockpot. Heat to boiling. Turn burner off, keep tightly covered, and let sit 1 hour. Add ham bone, onion, celery, and carrot; heat to boiling again, and simmer for 1½–2 hours until tender. Add all seasonings about 10 minutes before end of cooking time, stirring well. Remove bone, trim off meat, and add back to soup. Serves 10–12.

Note: May use ¼ pound bacon ends instead of ham bone.

Editor's Extra: After using all the slices of a bone-in ham, it's good to save the ham bone for various dishes like this delicious bean soup. Just wrap ham bone in foil and slip in freezer bag . . . it will keep several weeks.

Mennonite Country-Style Recipes & Kitchen Secrets (Pennsylvania)

I've learned that people will forget what you said, people will forget what you did, but people will never forget how you made them feel.
    —Maya Angelou

Vegetable Beef Soup

Vegetable Beef Soup

Now, this is what I call soup! With hot cornbread on the side, it's a heck of a meal.

1 pound soup meat
1 large meaty soup bone
3 quarts water
1 quart canned tomatoes
1½ cups ketchup, or 1 (6-ounce) can tomato paste
4 medium onions, chopped
2 large carrots, chopped or sliced
4 large potatoes, chopped
2 stalks celery, chopped
2 cups chopped cabbage
½ cup chopped green bell pepper
1 cup cut green beans
½ cup sliced okra
2 cups whole-kernel corn
2 cups green peas
1 teaspoon sugar
1 teaspoon seasoned salt (Lawry's)
1 teaspoon onion powder
1 teaspoon garlic powder
1 teaspoon Ac'cent (optional)
1 teaspoon salt, or more, to taste

Braise soup meat and soup bone in large heavy stockpot. Add water, tomatoes, and ketchup or tomato paste to pot. Stir to mix well, and bring to a boil. Cook until meat is tender.

Remove bone and soup meat. Chop meat, and discard bone. Add all vegetables except corn and peas. Simmer 1 hour.

Add corn, peas, spices, and chopped meat. Simmer 10 minutes longer. Taste; add additional salt, if necessary. If soup is too thick, add additional water. Freezes well. Makes 1½ gallons.

Editor's Extra: Lovers of spicy soup might add a can of Ro-Tel tomatoes, or red or black pepper.

Mrs. Rowe's Favorite Recipes (Virginia)

Worries go down better with soup.
—Jewish Proverb

Taco Soup

A satisfying soup you are sure to make again and again.

1 pound ground beef
1 (15-ounce) can pinto beans,
  drained
1 (15-ounce) can whole-kernel
  corn, drained
1 (15-ounce) can green beans,
  drained

1 (15-ounce) can chili starter
1 (15-ounce) can stewed tomatoes
1 (12-ounce) can beer
1 (10-ounce) can diced tomatoes
  with green chiles
1½ ounces taco seasoning mix
1 ounce ranch dressing mix

Brown meat in a big pot, and drain. Add drained vegetables; mix well. Add remaining ingredients, and bring to a boil. Simmer 30 minutes. Serves 6–8.

Editor's Extra: The alcohol in the beer cooks out, but water can be used instead.

Bountiful Blessings (Virginia)

Chicken Enchilada Soup

A thoughtful revision to a favorite soup.

1 onion, chopped
1 clove garlic, minced
4 boneless, skinless chicken
  breasts, boiled, cubed, and
  liquid reserved
2 tablespoons extra virgin
  olive oil
1 (16-ounce) can diced tomatoes

1 (10-ounce) can original
  Ro-Tel tomatoes
2 cups gluten-free beef broth
2 cups gluten-free chicken broth
2 teaspoons chili powder
Black pepper to taste
8 corn tortillas, cut into strips
1 (16-ounce) Mexican Velveeta

In a large soup pot, sauté onion, garlic, and cubed, cooked chicken in the oil. Add tomatoes, broths, 1 cup reserved cooking liquid, and spices. Cover; bring to a boil. Reduce heat, and simmer for 1 hour, stirring occasionally. Add tortilla strips to soup, and stir. Cut Velveeta into 1-inch cubes, and add to soup. Mix well. Simmer, uncovered, for about 10 minutes. Serve hot with crispy tortilla chips. Serves 8–10.

The Sun and the Rain & the Appleseed (Virginia)

Beef Stew Bourguignonne

A lot of the taste, but a lot easier than original Beef Bourguignonne.

2 pounds beef stew meat, cut in
   1-inch cubes
2 tablespoons oil
1 (10¾-ounce) can condensed
   golden mushroom soup
½ cup chopped onion
½ cup shredded carrots
⅓ cup dry red wine

1 (3-ounce) can chopped
   mushrooms, drained
¼ teaspoon crushed, dried
   oregano
¼ teaspoon Worcestershire
½ cup cold water
¼ cup all-purpose flour
Hot cooked noodles

In skillet, brown meat in hot oil; drain. Transfer meat to slow cooker. Stir in soup, onion, carrots, wine, mushrooms, oregano, and Worcestershire. Cover; cook on LOW heat setting for 12 hours.

   Turn cooker to HIGH heat setting. In a small measuring cup, blend cold water slowly into flour; stir into beef mixture. Cook and stir until thickened and bubbly. Serve stew over noodles. Serves 6.

Recipes from the Kitchens of Family & Friends (Oregon)

After Church Stew

1½ pounds lean stew beef,
   cut in 1-inch cubes
2 teaspoons salt
¼ teaspoon pepper
½ teaspoon basil
2 stalks celery, cut in ½-inch
   diagonal slices
4 medium carrots, pared and
   quartered

2 medium onions, cut in
   ½-inch thick slices and
   separated into rings
1 (10¾-ounce) can tomato
   soup
½ soup can water
3 medium potatoes, pared and
   cubed

Place beef cubes (no need to brown them) in a 3-quart casserole. Sprinkle evenly with salt, pepper, and basil. Top with celery, carrots, and onions. Combine soup and water; pour over meat and vegetables, coating all pieces. Cover tightly, and bake at 300° for 3 hours. Add potatoes, and bake an additional 45 minutes. Serves 6.

The Clovia Recipe Collection (Minnesota)

Monday's Chicken Chili

A delightful change from traditional chili . . . any day of the week.

3 tablespoons extra virgin
  olive oil
1 large onion, chopped
1 red bell pepper, chopped
1 green bell pepper, chopped
1 yellow bell pepper, chopped
1 jalapeño, seeded and minced
2 tablespoons minced garlic
2 tablespoons chili powder
1 teaspoon cumin
¼ teaspoon coriander

¼ teaspoon cinnamon
4 cups shredded cooked chicken
2 (28-ounce) cans diced Italian
  plum tomatoes, undrained
1 (15-ounce) can dark red kidney
  beans, drained and rinsed
1 tablespoon lemon juice
Salt and pepper to taste
Hot cooked rice or barley
Shredded cheese, sour cream, and
  chopped scallions for topping

Heat olive oil in a large heavy stockpot. Cook onion, bell peppers, and jalapeño chile in the hot oil for 5 minutes, stirring frequently. Stir in garlic. Cook until vegetables are tender, stirring constantly. Mix chili powder, cumin, coriander, and cinnamon in a bowl. Add spice mixture to stockpot, and mix well. Cook until slightly fragrant, stirring constantly.

Combine chicken, undrained tomatoes, beans, and lemon juice in a bowl, and mix well. Add chicken mixture to stockpot, and mix again. Season with salt and pepper. Simmer 15 minutes, stirring occasionally. Ladle over hot cooked rice or barley in chili bowls. Serve with shredded cheese, sour cream, and chopped scallions. Serves 8.

Provisions & Politics (Tennessee)

The informality of family life is a blessed condition that allows us to become our best while looking our worst.
—Marge Kennedy

Monday's Chicken Chili

Italian Beef Hoagies

Put in a slow cooker when you leave for work, and you'll be welcomed home by this inviting aroma.

1 (4-pound) boneless sirloin tip
  roast, halved
2 envelopes Italian salad
  dressing mix

2 cups water
1 (16-ounce) jar mild pepper
  rings, undrained
18 hoagie buns, split

Place roast in a slow cooker. Combine salad dressing mix and water; pour over roast. Cover, and cook on LOW for 8 hours, or until meat is tender. Remove meat; shred with a fork, and return to slow cooker. Add pepper rings with juice, and heat through. Spoon ½ cup meat mixture onto each bun. Makes 18 hoagies.

Come and Discover Special Appetites (Michigan)

Italian Beef

This is crowd-pleasing yummy. The peppers spark the wonderful flavor.

3½ pounds rump roast
4 cups hot water
4 beef bouillon cubes
1½ teaspoons salt
1 teaspoon pepper

2 dashes garlic salt
1½ teaspoons oregano
2 green bell peppers, cut into
  strips
2 tablespoons butter

Brown roast at 450° for 30 minutes. Mix remaining ingredients, except peppers and butter. Pour mixture over browned meat. Cover, and bake at 350° for 3 hours. Refrigerate in pan overnight.

  Brown bell peppers in butter. After browning, cover and steam for about 20 minutes. Pour bell peppers into juice around meat, slice meat very thinly, and put into juice. Reheat, and serve on buns. Makes about 15 sandwiches. If there are leftovers, you may have to add 1 cup beef bouillon when reheating.

Five Loaves and Two Fishes II (Illinois)

Best Ever Sloppy Joes

Great flavor.

1 (14-ounce) can petite-diced tomatoes	1 cup chopped yellow onion
⅓ cup red wine vinegar	1 cup chopped celery
1⅓ cups ketchup	½ cup chopped bell pepper
2–3 tablespoons brown sugar	3 garlic cloves, diced
1½ pounds ground sirloin	1–2 tablespoons chili powder
	1 teaspoon diced leaf oregano

Mix together tomatoes, vinegar, ketchup, and brown sugar until sugar is dissolved; set aside. Brown meat together with remaining ingredients. Drain, and add to tomato mixture in a Dutch oven. Cook over medium heat 10–15 minutes. Serve on buns. Makes about 5½ cups.

Taste of Clarkston: Tried & True Recipes (Michigan)

Pulled Pork

Need a delicious, super-easy dinner? Try this! Serve with hamburger buns or rolls and additional barbecue sauce.

2 large onions, sliced, divided	1 cup ginger ale
1 (4-pound) pork roast, shoulder or butt	1 (18-ounce) bottle barbecue sauce (your choice)

Place 1 sliced onion in crockpot. Place roast on top, and cover with remaining onion slices. Pour ginger ale over, cover, and cook on LOW about 12 hours. Remove roast; strain liquid, saving onions. Discard all liquid. Using 2 forks, shred meat; discard any remaining fat, bones, or skin. Return shredded meat and onions to crockpot, stir in barbecue sauce, and continue to cook another 4–6 hours on LOW. Serves 8–10.

Tip: Leftovers freeze well. Place a scoop of meat on a bun, and wrap really well. To reheat, remove wrapping, wrap in a paper towel, and microwave 1–2 minutes.

Bountiful Blessings (Virginia)

French Toasted Ham Sandwiches

So pretty . . . browned in butter.

12 slices firm textured white or rye bread
Mustard
6 thin slices cooked ham
6 thin slices Swiss cheese
6 slices chicken

2 eggs, slightly beaten
½ cup milk
½ teaspoon salt
Dash of black pepper
3–4 tablespoons butter

Spread each slice of bread with mustard. Make 6 sandwiches using 1 slice of ham, cheese, and chicken in each. Combine eggs, milk, salt, and pepper in a shallow dish. Dip each sandwich in egg mixture, turning to coat on both sides. Brown sandwiches in butter over low heat. Serves 6.

Little Bit Different! (Georgia)

inner Conversation Starters:

- *What three people, living or dead, would you want to invite to dinner?*

- *If you could only have five foods for the rest of your life, what would they be?*

- *What musical instrument would you like to be able to play, and why?*

Dinner Dishes

The Lunch Bell Chicken Pot Pie

More special than your usual chicken pot pie because of the puff pastry crust—this is a mainstay makeover that will knock your socks off. Man, it's good!

Puff pastry, cut into desired
  shape
1 egg, beaten
½ cup chopped onion
½ stick butter
½ cup all-purpose flour
¼ teaspoon black pepper

2 stalks celery, sliced
3 carrots, sliced
5½ cups chicken stock, divided
Salt to taste
3 cups cooked and cubed chicken
½ (16-ounce) bag frozen mixed
  vegetables

Preheat oven to 375°. Bring puff pastry to room temperature. Place on an ungreased cookie sheet. Brush with beaten egg, and let set for 30 minutes. Place in oven, and brush with beaten egg every 5 minutes for 20 minutes, or until golden brown; set aside.

In a large skillet, sauté onion in butter over medium heat until translucent. Add flour and pepper, and stir until well blended. Cook about 10 minutes on low heat, stirring occasionally.

While sauce is thickening, in a medium saucepan, sauté celery and carrots in ½ cup chicken stock until partially done, about 15 minutes. Drain; set aside. Slowly add remaining stock to flour mixture, stirring constantly with a wire whisk. Cook on medium heat until thickened, stirring often. Check for seasoning, and add salt, if necessary. Add cooked chicken, celery, and carrots. Add uncooked mixed vegetables, and stir gently. Cook until vegetables are heated.

Cut puff pastry in half, lengthwise. Place ½ of pastry in a baking dish. Put a large scoop of pot pie mixture on top of pastry; top with other half of pastry. Serves 6–8.

Favorites from the Lunch Bell (Virginia)

---

*If you can't get rid of the family skeleton,
you may as well make it dance.*
    —George Bernard Shaw, *Immaturity*

Chicken Casserole

Fix this one day, and bake it the next. Great for overnight guests.

1 large package chicken Stove Top Dressing	1½ cups mayonnaise
1 stick butter, melted	¾ teaspoon salt
1 cup water	2 eggs
1 chicken, cooked and cubed	1½ cups milk
¼ cup chopped green onions (including tops)	1 (10¾-ounce) can cream of chicken soup
	1 cup grated Cheddar cheese

Mix dressing with butter and water. Put ½ of mixture in greased 9x13-inch casserole. Mix chicken with green onions, mayonnaise, and salt. Put over dressing mixture in pan. Top with remaining dressing mixture. Beat eggs; add milk; pour over dressing mixture. Cover with foil, refrigerate overnight.

Before baking, spread cream of chicken soup over top. Bake, uncovered, 30 minutes at 350°. Sprinkle grated cheese over top. Bake 10 minutes more. Cut in squares, and serve. Serves 10.

A Collection of Recipes from St. Matthew Lutheran Church (Illinois)

Hot Chicken Salad

2 cups chopped celery	1 tablespoon lemon juice
2 cups cooked, cubed chicken	1 cup mayonnaise (Duke's), plus or minus a little
½ cup coarsely chopped cashews	1 cup shredded Cheddar cheese
1 tablespoon minced onion	1 cup crushed potato chips
⅛ teaspoon salt	½ cup seasoned bread crumbs

Preheat oven to 350°. Mix together celery, chicken, cashews, onion, salt, and lemon juice. Add mayonnaise until moist. Pour into a greased 9x13-inch casserole dish. Sprinkle cheese over top of casserole. In a separate bowl, combine potato chips and bread crumbs. Sprinkle potato chip and bread crumb mixture on top, covering all of the cheese. Bake for 20–30 minutes until hot and brown. Serve immediately. Serves 4.

Favorites from the Lunch Bell (Virginia)

Broccoli and Chicken Casserole

There's a good reason this is an old favorite.

20 ounces chopped broccoli, cooked, drained

1 large chicken (or 4–5 boneless breasts), cooked, cubed

Spread broccoli in greased 9x13-inch baking dish. Top with chicken.

SAUCE:

1 cup shredded sharp Cheddar cheese
2 (10¾-ounce) cans cream of chicken soup
1 cup mayonnaise

1 tablespoon lemon juice
½ teaspoon curry powder (optional)
Buttered crumbs, to cover casserole

Combine cheese, soup, mayonnaise, lemon juice, and curry powder, if desired; spread over chicken and broccoli. Sprinkle crumbs over top. Bake at 350° for 30–45 minutes, or until top is browned. Serves 4–6.

90th Anniversary Trinity Lutheran Church Cookbook (Great Plains)

Cheesy Turkey Bake

Your company will gobble this up! Two pies serve a bunch.

3 cups diced, cooked turkey
2 cups cooked rice
1 medium onion, chopped
½ cup chopped celery
1 (10¾-ounce) can cream of mushroom soup
1 (15-ounce) can mixed vegetables, drained

1 cup mayonnaise
4 tablespoons lemon juice
2 teaspoons salt
1 cup grated smokey Cheddar cheese
2 (9-inch) deep-dish pie shells
4 tablespoons butter, melted
2 cups crushed cornflakes

In large bowl, mix all ingredients except pie shells, butter, and cornflakes. Refrigerate overnight or several hours.

Bake unfilled pie shells at 400° for 10 minutes. Fill pie shells with turkey mixture, and bake at 350° for 40 minutes. Melt butter, and sauté cornflakes. Sprinkle this topping over pies, and bake 5 more minutes. Each pie serves 6.

Dawn to Dusk (Ohio)

Broccoli and Chicken Casserole

Mom's Chicken Spaghetti

An old family favorite kicked up a notch, and packed with flavor.

6 chicken breasts, or
  1 small fryer
¾ cup chopped onion
1 cup chopped celery
½ cup chopped green bell
  pepper
1 stick butter
1 (15-ounce) can diced tomatoes
1 cup water
2 teaspoons salt
1 tablespoon hot sauce
½ teaspoon red pepper
1 (8-ounce) can sliced
  mushrooms, drained
1 (10¾-ounce) can cream of
  mushroom soup
Ripe olives (¼ cup) (optional)
1 pound Velveeta cheese
1 (12-ounce) package angel hair
  pasta

Boil chicken till cooked; remove meat from bones, and save broth for cooking pasta.

In Dutch oven, sauté onion, celery, and bell pepper in butter. Add remaining ingredients, except Velveeta and pasta; mix well. Cut Velveeta into chunks, and stir into mixture till melted.

Cook pasta in chicken broth. Layer pasta and sauce in a lightly greased casserole dish. Heat at 350° for about 30 minutes, or till bubbly. This dish can be made ahead of time and heated just before serving. Casserole can also be frozen. Serves 6–8.

Sensational Seafood Recipes and More! (Virginia)

There is no sight on earth more appealing than the sight of a woman making dinner for someone she loves.
—Thomas Wolfe

Chicken Tetrazzini Glencrest

Casual and hearty, this is a tried-and-true people pleaser.

1 (5½- to 6-pound) hen	Salt and pepper to taste
6 tablespoons butter, divided	1 onion, chopped
4 tablespoons flour	½ green bell pepper, chopped
2 cups hot chicken broth	1 pound mushrooms, sliced
1½ cups whipping cream	½ pound thin spaghetti
¼ cup sherry	1 cup grated Parmesan cheese
1 teaspoon lemon juice	

Simmer hen in water to cover until tender; let cool in broth. Pull skin from hen, and slip meat from bones. Chill meat, then dice. Reserve broth.

Melt 4 tablespoons butter over low heat; add flour, stirring 3–4 minutes until well blended. Slowly stir in 2 cups reserved broth, cream, and sherry. Season with lemon juice, salt and pepper. Simmer and stir sauce with a wire whisk until thick, smooth, and hot.

Sauté onion, bell pepper, and mushrooms in remaining 2 tablespoons butter. Add to sauce. Cook spaghetti as directed, using any leftover broth. Place spaghetti in bottom of a greased 9x13-inch baking dish; cover with chicken and sauce. Sprinkle with Parmesan cheese. Bake at 325° for 30 minutes until bubbly. Serves 8–10.

Bluegrass Winners (Kentucky)

As a child, my family's menu consisted of two choices: "Take it, or leave it."
—Buddy Hackett

Plucky Enchiladas

A good after-Thanksgiving recipe for leftover turkey. You'll want to make it often.

2 (4-ounce) cans whole green
  chiles
1 large garlic clove, minced
½ cup and 2 tablespoons
  vegetable oil, divided
1 (l-pound, 12-ounce) can
  whole tomatoes
2 cups chopped onions

1 teaspoon salt
½ teaspoon oregano
3 cups cooked and shredded
  turkey or chicken
2 cups sour cream
½ pound Cheddar cheese,
  grated
12–16 corn tortillas

Rinse seeds from chiles, and chop. Sauté chiles and garlic in 2 table-spoons oil. Drain tomatoes, reserving ½ cup liquid. Break up toma-toes, and add to sautéed chiles and garlic along with onions, salt, oregano, and reserved ½ cup tomato liquid. Simmer slowly, uncov-ered, until thick, about 30 minutes. Set aside.

Combine turkey or chicken with sour cream and cheese. Heat ½ cup remaining oil, and fry tortillas until limp. Drain on paper towels. Fill each tortilla with meat mixture, and roll up. Place seam down in ungreased casserole dish, and pour sauce on top. Bake at 350° for 20 minutes. Freezable. Serves 6.

Editor's Extra: Make it easier: Buy diced green chiles; use jarred minced gar-lic; use diced canned tomatoes; use frozen chopped onion; use already shred-ded Cheddar cheese.

With Hands & Heart Cookbook (Missouri)

Life is what happens to you while you're busy making other plans. —Allen Saunders

Sour Cream Enchiladas

An excellent family-time-together dinner.

1 pound ground beef
½ cup chopped onion
1 teaspoon garlic powder
1 teaspoon cumin
½ teaspoon salt
1 tablespoon chili powder
2 (10¾-ounce) cans cream of
  mushroom soup

¾ cup milk
1 (16-ounce) carton sour cream
8 flour tortillas
2 cups shredded sharp Cheddar
  cheese
1 (4¼-ounce) can sliced black
  olives

Cook beef and onion until beef is browned and onion is translucent. Drain. Stir in garlic powder, cumin, salt, and chili powder; set aside.

Combine soup and milk, and cook until bubbly. Remove from heat, and add sour cream, stirring until well combined. Set aside.

Warm and soften tortillas briefly in microwave or on grill. Lay each tortilla flat, and place 2 tablespoons (or more) beef mixture down center of each. Sprinkle each with 1 tablespoon (or more) cheese, and fold over, tucking in ends. Place in a buttered glass baking dish that has a thin layer of sour cream mixture in bottom. Pour remaining sour cream mixture over all, and bake at 350° for 25 minutes. Sprinkle with more shredded cheese and olive slices, and bake 5 minutes more. Serves 4–6.

Recipes Tried and True (Idaho)

This is part of what a family is about, not just love. It's knowing that your family will be there watching out for you. Nothing else will give you that. Not money. Not fame. Not work.
—Mitch Albom, *Tuesdays with Morrie*

Lasagna

Lasagna

A masterful mix of a classic dish.

1 pound ground beef
2–3 (8-ounce) cans tomato sauce
2 (6-ounce) cans tomato paste
2 teaspoons Italian seasoning
1 teaspoon oregano
½ teaspoon garlic salt
9 lasagna noodles

3 cups ricotta or cottage cheese
2 eggs
1 teaspoon salt
¼ teaspoon pepper
2 tablespoons parsley flakes
1 pound shredded mozzarella cheese

Brown beef, and drain. Add tomato sauce and paste, Italian seasoning, oregano, and garlic salt; simmer 30 minutes. In large pot, cook noodles in water to cover; drain. In bowl, combine remaining ingredients, except mozzarella cheese.

In a greased 9x13-inch baking dish or pan, make layers of noodles, meat sauce, ricotta cheese sauce, and mozzarella cheese. Repeat until all ingredients are used (2 or 3 layers). Bake at 375° for 35 minutes. Serves 6.

Cookin' with the Colts (West Virginia)

Spaghetti Pie

A go-to recipe for guaranteed enjoyment.

6 ounces uncooked spaghetti
2 tablespoons butter
⅓ cup grated Parmesan cheese
2 eggs, well beaten
1 pound ground beef

½ cup chopped onion
½ (26-ounce) jar spaghetti sauce
1 cup cottage cheese
½ cup shredded mozzarella cheese

Cook spaghetti until tender; drain. Stir in butter, Parmesan cheese, and eggs. Form crust of spaghetti in lightly greased 8x8-inch pan or large pie pan. Cook ground beef and onion, and add spaghetti sauce. Top spaghetti crust with cottage cheese. Add meat mixture. Bake at 350° for 45 minutes. Top with mozzarella cheese, and return to oven until cheese melts. Serves 4–5.

Lutheran Church Women Cookbook (Iowa)

Romanoff Beef Noodle Casserole

This is a good casserole for big parties as it doubles beautifully. Serve with a green salad and French bread.

1 pound lean ground beef	8 ounces fine egg noodles
1 onion, chopped	4 ounces cream cheese, softened
1 clove garlic, minced	⅔ cup sour cream
1 teaspoon salt	6 scallions, chopped
Pepper to taste	½ cup grated Cheddar cheese
1 (15-ounce) can tomato sauce	

Preheat oven to 350°. In medium skillet, brown beef, onion, and garlic. Break meat up as it cooks. Pour off excess fat. Add salt and pepper to taste. Add tomato sauce, and simmer uncovered for 15 minutes.

While sauce mixture simmers, cook noodles according to package directions. Do not overcook noodles. Drain.

In a small bowl, blend cream cheese, sour cream, and scallions. Place ⅓ of cream sauce and ⅓ of noodles in greased 2-quart casserole. Top with ⅓ of meat sauce. Repeat layers twice, using all noodles, cream sauce, and meat sauce mixture. Top with grated Cheddar cheese.

At this point, dish can be frozen or refrigerated. If frozen, thaw before baking. Bake at 350° for 30 minutes, until hot and bubbly. Serves 8.

Sharing Our Best (New York)

No one's family is normal. Normalcy is a lie invented by advertising agencies to make the rest of us feel inferior.
—Claire LaZebnik, *Epic Fail*

Make-Ahead Macaroni Frankfurter Bake

A great spoon-it-up meal everybody enjoys, especially the kids.

6 slices bacon
5 frankfurters, divided
¾ cup sliced celery
½ cup chopped onion
2 tablespoons bacon fat
1 tablespoon flour
½ teaspoon salt

½ teaspoon pepper
1 (10½-ounce) can cream of
  celery soup
1 (12-ounce) can evaporated milk
3 cups hot cooked macaroni
½ cup grated Cheddar cheese

Fry bacon crisp; reserve 2 tablespoons fat. Slice 3 frankfurters. Sauté sliced frankfurters, celery, and onion in reserved bacon fat. Stir in flour, salt, and pepper. Add soup and milk. Cook 10 minutes until slightly thickened, stirring constantly. Crumble bacon; add to sauce. Alternate layers of macaroni and cream sauce mixture in a greased 1½-quart casserole. Split remaining 2 frankfurters lengthwise. Place on top of casserole. Top with cheese. Bake in moderate 350° oven for 20–25 minutes. Serves 6–8.

Goodies and Guess-Whats (Colorado)

Ham and Cheese Noodle Casserole

1 (8-ounce) package wide
  noodles
2½ cups diced cooked ham
2 cups shredded Swiss cheese
⅓ cup chopped green bell
  pepper

2 tablespoons chopped onion
1 teaspoon salt
1 cup sour cream
Bell pepper rings for garnish
  (optional)

Cook noodles according to package directions; drain. Toss together noodles, ham, cheese, bell pepper, onion, and salt in large bowl. Blend in sour cream. Pour into greased 2-quart casserole. Bake at 375° for 25–30 minutes, or till cheese melts and casserole is heated through. Top with bell pepper rings, if desired. Serves 6.

Culinary Crinkles (South Carolina)

Dinner in a Skillet

Dinner in a Skillet

A cornbread-topped meal in a skillet that is just waiting to be tapped into!

1 pound ground beef
Salt and pepper to taste
1 onion, diced
1 medium bell pepper, diced
1 (10-ounce) can Ro-Tel
  tomatoes
1 (15-ounce) can pinto beans or
  Ranch Style Beans
1 (15-ounce) can cream-style
  corn
1 (15-ounce) can whole-kernel
  corn
1 package cornbread mix

Brown ground beef in large skillet; drain, then season with salt and pepper. Add onion, bell pepper, tomatoes, beans, and corn. Stir to combine. Cook on high heat until mixture starts to boil. Remove from heat. If skillet is not ovenproof, transfer to baking dish.

Mix cornbread according to package directions. Spoon mixture over ground beef mixture, completely covering to make a top crust. Do not stir. Bake in 350° oven until cornbread is golden brown. Serves 6–8.

Cooking with Miracle Deliverance (South Carolina)

Skillet Macaroni Dinner

Easy, breezy, pleasy.

1 pound ground beef
1 tablespoon oil
1 medium onion, chopped
1 (15-ounce) can diced tomatoes
1 (8-ounce) can corn, undrained
½ cup uncooked macaroni
1 teaspoon chili powder
1 teaspoon garlic salt
½ cup shredded Cheddar cheese

Brown beef in oil. Add onion, tomatoes, corn, and macaroni, and cook for 30 minutes, or till macaroni is tender; stir occasionally. Add chili powder and garlic salt; stir. Place cheese on top. Heat, covered, 5 minutes. Serves 4.

Bountiful Blessings (Virginia)

Husband's Delight

Mine, for sure!

1 (8-ounce) package cream
  cheese, softened
2 cups sour cream
3 green onions and tops,
  chopped
1½ pounds ground beef
2 tablespoons butter

2 (8-ounce) cans tomato sauce
1 teaspoon sugar
1 teaspoon salt
Dash of pepper
Dash of Worcestershire
10 ounces noodles
½ cup shredded cheese

In a bowl, mix cream cheese, sour cream, and onions; set aside. Brown beef in butter; add tomato sauce, sugar, salt, pepper and Worcestershire. Cook noodles according to package directions. In a 2-quart casserole dish, alternate layers of noodles, beef mixture, and sour cream mixture. Top with shredded cheese, and bake at 350° until brown and cheese is melted. Serves 8.

Keepers (Texas)

Cabbage Casserole

Easy, cheesy, and delicious!

1 pound ground beef
1 pound bulk seasoned sausage
1 medium onion, diced
1 medium bell pepper, diced
1 stalk celery, thinly sliced
2 garlic cloves, crushed
1 cup cooked rice
¼ cup water

2 (10-ounce) cans Ro-Tel diced
  tomatoes with green chiles
1 medium head cabbage, coarsely
  shredded
16 ounces Velveeta cheese
½ stick butter or margarine
1 tablespoon flour
1 cup milk

Brown beef and sausage in Dutch oven. Drain fat; add onion, pepper, celery, garlic, and rice. Cook 5 minutes. Add water, tomatoes, and cabbage; cook 10 minutes. Pour into a 9x13-inch baking dish.

In separate bowl, microwave cheese and butter until melted. Stir in flour and milk. Pour over meat mixture. Cover, and bake at 350° for 45 minutes. Uncover, and bake 15 minutes more. Serve with cornbread. This recipe freezes well.

Treasures from Our Kitchen (Mississippi)

Tostada Pizza

A taco-flavored pizza—what's not to love!

2 tablespoons cornmeal
2 cups Bisquick
1¼ cups cold water, divided
1 pound ground beef
1 package taco seasoning mix

1 (16-ounce) can refried beans
1 cup shredded cheese
Chopped lettuce, tomato, onion,
  chiles, olives, etc., for toppings

Grease 12-inch pizza pan. Sprinkle with cornmeal. In bowl, combine Bisquick and ½ cup cold water. Stir with fork to combine. Turn out onto lightly floured surface, and knead 5–6 times. Roll to 14-inch circle, and put into pan, crimping edges.

In skillet, brown meat; drain. Stir in ¾ cup water and taco seasoning. Reduce heat, and simmer 15 minutes. Spread refried beans on the dough, and top with meat mixture. Bake at 450° for 18–20 minutes. Top with cheese, and bake another 3–4 minutes. Serve with your choice of toppings. Serves 4–6.

Tastes from the Country (Idaho)

Southwestern Tamale Pie

One word . . . mmmmm.

1 pound ground beef
1 small onion, diced
1 (10¾-ounce) can cream of
  chicken soup
1 (10¾-ounce) can golden
  mushroom soup

1 cup evaporated milk
½ cup taco sauce
1½ cups chopped green chiles
1 dozen corn tortillas
1½ cups grated Cheddar or
  Monterey Jack cheese

Brown meat with onion in large skillet; drain excess fat. Add soups, milk, taco sauce, and green chiles. Simmer all ingredients together about 10 minutes. Cut corn tortillas into strips. (Tortillas do not need to be fried.) Layer on bottom of 2-quart casserole dish with meat mixture and cheese; continue alternating layers; top layer should end with cheese. Cover casserole, and bake at 350° for 1 hour. Serves 5–6.

Editor's Extra: May sub 3 cups diced chicken for beef.

Comida Sabrosa (New Mexico)

Shrimp Pesto Pizza

Okay, we know using a prepared pizza dough is cheating, but when time is of the essence, it surely comes in handy! Use freshly made pesto to really bring out the aromas and flavor of the basil.

6 jumbo shrimp, halved
   lengthwise (or 12 medium),
   peeled
¼ cup homemade basil pesto,
   divided
¼ cup sliced sun-dried
   tomatoes, packed in oil,
   drained, reserve oil
3 garlic cloves, sliced

1 cup sliced mushrooms
¼ cup sliced roasted red bell
   pepper
1 prepared pizza shell
½ cup grated mozzarella cheese,
   divided
¼ cup snipped fresh spinach
   leaves
2 tablespoons pine nuts

Toss shrimp with 1 tablespoon pesto, and set aside. Drain about 2 teaspoons oil from sun-dried tomatoes into a small skillet. Heat oil over medium-high heat, and sauté garlic, mushrooms, sun-dried tomatoes, and roasted pepper for 5 minutes. Remove from heat.

Place a pizza stone in the oven and preheat to 425°. Spread the remaining pesto over pizza shell. Sprinkle with half the cheese. Top with sauté mixture, and sprinkle with half the remaining cheese. Place pizza on the stone, and bake 8–10 minutes. Remove from oven, and arrange shrimp on top of pizza.

Return to oven, and bake for 3 minutes, or until shrimp start to curl. Remove from oven, and set to broil. Sprinkle with spinach, pine nuts, and remaining cheese, and set under broiler for 1–2 minutes, or until cheese is just bubbly. Remove from oven, and let rest for 3–5 minutes before slicing. Serves 4.

Editor's Extra: If you don't have a pizza stone, a regular pizza pan will work. Jarred basil pesto can be substituted for the homemade.

Aromatherapy in the Kitchen (Utah)

It's the sense of what family is at the dinner table. It was the joy of knowing mother was in the kitchen making our favorite dish. I wish more people would do this and recall the joy of life.
   —Paul Prudhomme

Shrimp Pesto Pizza

Shrimp Boil Dinner

With a salad, this is a complete meal for a fun supper party.

2 packages crab boil	20 new potatoes
6 lemons, halved	15 small onions
1 tablespoon Tabasco Sauce	10 ears corn, shucked and halved
2–3 tablespoons ice cream salt or kosher salt	6 pounds fresh unpeeled shrimp

In a large roaster half filled with water, bring the crab boil, lemons, Tabasco, and salt to a boil. Add new potatoes and onions, and boil until potatoes are tender. Add corn. When corn is tender, add shrimp. The shrimp are ready when they turn pink. This will take only a few minutes after the water has come to a full boil again. Drain, and serve. Serves 10 or more.

Encore! Nashville (Tennessee)

Instead of going out to dinner, buy good food. Cooking at home shows such affection. In a bad economy, it's more important to make yourself feel good.
—Ina Garten

Poultry & Seafood

Chicken Rolls

Easy to make, yet fancy enough for a special occasion.

4 boneless, skinless chicken
  breasts
3 ounces cream cheese, sliced
  thin

4 pieces ham, sliced thin
4 pieces Swiss cheese, sliced thin
4 pieces bacon

Flatten chicken between pieces of wax paper. Layer with cream cheese topped with ham and Swiss cheese, then roll up. Wrap a piece of bacon around each roll. Place seam side down in greased baking dish; bake at 350° for 1 hour.

CHEESE SAUCE:
½ stick butter
1 (10¾-ounce) can cream of
  mushroom soup

1 soup can of milk
1 cup grated Cheddar cheese
Pepper and garlic salt to taste

Melt butter in small saucepan over medium heat. Add soup and milk. When warm, add cheese, pan drippings from rolls, and pepper and garlic salt to taste. Heat through. Serve over chicken rolls. Serves 4.

Heart & Soul (Georgia)

Chicken in Lemon Sauce

Short on prep . . . long on tangy taste.

6 chicken breasts, skinned,
  boned, halved
½ cup butter
Salt and pepper to taste
2 teaspoons grated lemon rind

2 tablespoons lemon juice
2 tablespoons sherry (optional)
1 cup heavy cream
Parmesan cheese

In saucepan, sauté chicken in butter till light brown. Season with salt and pepper. Place in 9x13-inch greased baking dish. Add lemon rind, lemon juice, and sherry, if desired, to butter left in saucepan. Cook and stir a few minutes. Check seasoning. Stir constantly, slowly adding cream to sauce. Remove from heat, and pour over chicken. Sprinkle cheese over top, and bake at 350° for 20–30 minutes. Serves 6.

The Cooking Book (Kentucky)

Best Ever Chicken

Mushroom lovers will relish this tomato-y chicken dish that bursts with flavor.

4 whole skinless, boneless,
   chicken breasts
½ pound sliced mushrooms, or
   more, if desired
1 (14½-ounce) can crushed,
   stewed, or diced tomatoes

½ cup Italian or Russian
   salad dressing
1 (1¾-ounce) envelope dry onion
   soup mix
1 bay leaf

Place chicken breasts in a baking dish; top with sliced mushrooms. Pour tomatoes over mushrooms. Mix dressing with onion soup mix, and pour over. Tuck in bay leaf. Bake, uncovered, at 350° for 1 hour, basting frequently. Serve with rice or noodles. If too much liquid, drain some prior to serving. Remove bay leaf before serving. Serves 4–6.

Where There's a Will... (Mid-Atlantic)

Honey French Chicken

This recipe won second prize in the North Carolina Chicken Cooking Contest.

6 chicken breasts
1 teaspoon MSG flavor
   enhancer (optional)
½ cup corn oil
½ cup honey
¼ cup cider vinegar

¼ cup chili sauce
1 tablespoon Worcestershire
½ (1¾-ounce) envelope dry onion
   soup mix
¼ teaspoon salt

Sprinkle chicken with flavor enhancer, if desired. In a jar, place oil, honey, vinegar, chili sauce, Worcestershire, soup mix, and salt; shake well. Place chicken in single layer in large shallow baking pan. Pour sauce over chicken. Bake, uncovered, at 350° for 35–40 minutes, basting occasionally. When done, fork can be inserted with ease. Serves 6.

Mountain Elegance (North Carolina)

Parmesan Oven-Fried Chicken

An easy entrée with a tasty salad dressing coating.

½ cup Italian bread crumbs
2 tablespoons parsley
¼ teaspoon black pepper
⅓ cup grated Parmesan
  cheese

¼ teaspoon garlic powder
6 chicken boneless, skinless
  chicken breast halves
¼–½ cup French salad dressing

Combine all ingredients, except chicken and salad dressing, in a large bag. Dip clean, dry chicken into salad dressing, then shake in mixture in bag. Place in a 9x13-inch pan. Bake 1 hour at 350°, uncovered. Serves 6.

A Taste of Fishers (Indiana)

Smothered Chicken

My New Orleans grandmother made this and served it over rice. Talk about good!—Gwen

1 (3-pound) fryer
Salt and pepper to taste
½ cup vegetable oil
½ cup all-purpose flour
1 cup chopped onions
1 cup chopped celery

3 garlic cloves, chopped
½ cup chopped green onions
  (reserve tops to garnish)
1 small bell pepper, chopped
1 quart water
1 cup chopped mushrooms

Cut fryer into serving pieces, and season with salt and pepper; set aside. In a heavy pot, make roux using oil and flour. Cook until brown. Add all vegetables except mushrooms. Sauté until done, about 15 minutes. Add chicken, and stir well. Cook approximately 20 minutes. Add water and mushrooms. Cover, and let simmer about 1 hour. Season to taste, and garnish with chopped green onion tops. Serves 6.

The Encyclopedia of Cajun and Creole Cuisine (Louisiana)

*Parmesan
Oven-Fried Chicken*

Down Home "Fried" Chicken

Definitely not your usual fried chicken. This is breaded and baked. Superb!

1 (3-pound) chicken, cut up
1 cup buttermilk
½ cup all-purpose flour
2 tablespoons chopped parsley
Salt and pepper to taste

1 teaspoon dried thyme
⅛ cup olive or vegetable oil
⅛ cup butter or margarine
¼ cup chicken broth

Marinate clean, dry chicken pieces in buttermilk in frig for 2 hours.

In a bowl, combine flour, parsley, salt, pepper, and thyme. Drain buttermilk into shallow baking dish (or discard, and use ½ cup fresh). Roll chicken pieces in flour mixture.

Heat oil and butter in skillet. Add chicken, and brown, a few pieces at a time, over medium heat. Place chicken on top of remaining buttermilk in baking dish. Add chicken broth to skillet. Scrape up brown bits, and pour around, not over, chicken. Bake, uncovered, at 375° until top is crisp and chicken is tender, about 50 minutes. Serves 6.

Down Home Cooking from Hocking County (Ohio)

Spicy Fried Chicken

This chicken is just a tad spicy . . . not too hot. Try it, you'll love it!

3 pounds chicken pieces, or
  1 (2½-pound) fryer, cut up
½ cup all-purpose flour
1 teaspoon salt or garlic salt
1 teaspoon dry mustard
1 teaspoon chili powder

1 teaspoon paprika
½ teaspoon cayenne pepper
¼ teaspoon freshly ground
  black pepper
Corn oil

Wash chicken and dry on paper towels. Combine flour and seasonings in a paper bag. Place chicken pieces, a few at a time, in bag, twist end, and shake vigorously to coat chicken well. Heat 1½ inches of oil in a deep skillet until temperature reaches 365°. Carefully lower chicken into hot oil, and cook 8–10 minutes on each side or until golden brown. Lift chicken out, and drain well on paper towels. Serves 4–6.

Loaves and Fishes (Alabama)

Chicken with Drop Dumplin's

This is just downright duh-licious!

1 (3- to 4-pound) chicken,
  cut up
2 stalks celery, diced
2 tablespoons chicken bouillon
  granules
1 bay leaf
8 cups water
2 cups all-purpose flour
4 teaspoons baking powder
1 teaspoon salt
¾ cup milk
½ cup chopped green onion tops
Pinch of cayenne pepper
½ cup chopped fresh parsley
¼ teaspoon freshly grated
  nutmeg
1 (10¾-ounce) can cream of
  chicken soup
Salt and pepper to taste

Place chicken pieces, celery, bouillon, and bay leaf in a stockpot. Add water, and bring to a boil over medium-high heat. Reduce heat, and cook for 45–60 minutes, or until chicken is tender. Remove chicken, and let it cool slightly. Pick meat off of the bones, discarding the bones and skin; set aside.

Sift flour, baking powder, and salt into a large bowl. Add milk, and mix well. Add onions and cayenne; mix. Drop batter by tablespoons into the boiling broth until all the batter is used up. Gently shake the pot. (Never stir dumplings with a spoon, as this will tear them.) Add parsley and nutmeg; shake pot again. Cover, reduce heat, and simmer gently for about 15 minutes without lifting the lid. While the dumplings are cooking, heat soup with 1 can water in a small saucepan. When dumplings are done, carefully pour the soup mixture into the dumpling pot. Shake the pot gently. Return chicken to the pot, and shake the pot again, this time in a rotating motion. Season to taste with salt and pepper. Serves 6–8.

Editor's Extra: Some people like strip dumplings made by rolling the dough out thinly on a heavily floured surface, then cutting into strips before dropping into the boiling broth. Either way, this is a best-loved family favorite in the South.

The Lady & Sons, Too! (Georgia)

Creamed Chicken and Biscuits

Creamed Chicken and Biscuits

Chicken . . . and biscuits . . combined—oh my goodness!

1½ teaspoons butter or
   margarine
½ large onion, chopped
¼ cup chopped celery
4 cups chopped cooked chicken
1 (10¾-ounce) can cream of
   chicken soup (undiluted)

1 cup sour cream
½ cup milk
½ teaspoon thyme
1 cup shredded mild Cheddar
   cheese, divided
6 frozen biscuits, thawed

Preheat oven to 350°. Grease bottom and sides of 7x11-inch baking dish. Melt butter in a small nonstick skillet over medium-high heat. Stir in onion and celery; sauté until tender. Combine sautéed onion and celery, chicken, soup, sour cream, milk, and seasonings in a medium bowl; mix well. Spoon mixture into prepared baking dish. Bake 15 minutes. Remove from oven. Sprinkle with ¾ cup Cheddar cheese. Arrange biscuits in a single layer over top. Sprinkle with remaining ¼ cup Cheddar cheese. Bake until biscuits are golden brown and the sauce is bubbly, about 20 minutes. Serve immediately. Serves 6.

Loving, Caring and Sharing (Virginia)

Creamy Crockpot Chicken

So flavorful and moist, you'll make this again and again.

1 cut-up chicken, or 4 boneless
   breasts
1 envelope dry Italian dressing
   mix

1 (8-ounce) package cream
   cheese, cubed
1 (10¾-ounce) can cream of
   chicken soup

Place all ingredients in crockpot on LOW for 8 hours or until chicken is done and gravy is smooth and creamy. Serve over cooked rice or mashed potatoes. Serves 6.

Note: This recipe is very flexible. If you like or need more gravy, add more soup; or try a different "cream of" soup variety; add more chicken. If you don't have Italian dressing mix, use another dry mix. I have tried lots of different combinations, and they have all been great.

Feeding the Flock (Nevada)

Chicken Taco Bake

Quick and easy!

1 pound chicken, cut into cubes	6 flour tortillas, cut into 1-inch
1 (15-ounce) can tomato soup	strips
1 cup salsa	1 cup shredded Cheddar cheese,
½ cup milk	divided
1 (16-ounce) can refried beans	

Preheat oven to 400°. In oiled skillet over medium heat, cook chicken until brown, and juices run clear; pour off fat. Add soup, salsa, milk, refried beans, tortilla strips, and ½ cup cheese. Spoon into a shallow 2-quart baking dish. Cover, and bake about 20 minutes, until hot. Sprinkle with remaining ½ cup cheese.

Kids in the Kitchen (Arizona)

Cranberry-Glazed Roast Turkey

An easy-do slow cooker recipe. Try this with Cornish game hens for a special dinner. . . makes for impressive individual servings.

1 (4-pound) turkey roast	1 teaspoon Worcestershire
1 (16-ounce) can whole or	¼ cup orange juice
jellied cranberry sauce	2 teaspoons grated orange rind
¼ cup butter or margarine,	⅛ teaspoon poultry seasoning
melted	2 teaspoons brown sugar

Place turkey roast in slow cooker. Mix together cranberry sauce, butter, Worcestershire, orange juice, orange rind, poultry seasoning, and brown sugar. Pour over turkey. Cover, and cook on LOW 8–10 hours. Baste turkey with cranberry glaze before removing turkey to warm platter to slice. Offer remaining cranberry glaze on the side for those who want extra. Serves 6.

Quick Crockery (Colorado)

Smoked Turkey Breast
with Herb Barbecue Sauce

Cooked in a pot on the grill slowly and deliciously. This turkey is great for dinner or sandwiches. Heck, it's good for picnics, tailgates, lunch boxes, etc.

½ cup butter or margarine
1 garlic clove, minced
1 medium onion, minced
¾ cup tarragon vinegar
1 teaspoon salt
Freshly ground black pepper
  to taste

3 tablespoons brown sugar
Sprigs of fresh rosemary, thyme,
  marjoram, and parsley,
  chopped, or 2 teaspoons dried
  herbs
1 (7- to 8-pound) turkey breast

To make barbecue sauce, combine all ingredients, except turkey, in a small saucepan, and simmer gently about 5 minutes. Place turkey in a roasting pan, and brush with sauce.

To grill over charcoal, cover pan loosely with a single sheet of foil, and grill over medium heat 2½ hours with grill covered. Remove foil, and baste again with barbecue sauce. Add damp hickory chips to fire, and continue cooking 1 hour in covered grill, basting occasionally with sauce.

To grill with a gas grill, add about 2 teaspoons liquid smoke seasoning to sauce. Follow instructions above for charcoal grilling, adding damp hickory chips for the last hour, if grill is suited for that.

To serve, slice turkey, and place on platter. Add remaining barbecue sauce to roasting pan drippings dissolved in a little water, and bring to a boil. Serve sauce on the side with turkey.

Heart of the Harbor (Virginia)

People are just as happy as they make up their minds to be.
—Abraham Lincoln

Grandmother's Turkey Hash on Waffles

This is a grandmother's recipe that has been used for 85 or more years at special family gatherings. It is a good use for leftover turkey.

4 tablespoons butter	**8 cups cooked, diced turkey**
½ cup all-purpose flour	**¼ cup chopped pimentos**
1 quart turkey or chicken stock	**¼ pound sliced mushrooms,**
½ tablespoon salt	**fresh or canned, drained**
¼ teaspoon pepper	**1½ tablespoons chopped parsley**
½ teaspoon paprika	**Waffles or patty shells, cooked**

In double boiler, melt butter, and slowly add flour to make a thick paste. Add turkey stock, stirring constantly to prevent lumping; cook till smooth. Season with salt, pepper, and paprika. Add remaining ingredients. (If fresh mushrooms are used, first sauté in additional melted butter till brown.) Heat thoroughly over boiling water and keep hot till ready to serve. Serve hash over cooked waffles or patty shells. May be prepared in advance. Serves 15.

Editor's Extra: Grandmothers today might use a whisk to prevent lumping, and it could be cooked in a heavy coated pot. A double boiler does keep it warm, and heats more gently, but if you don't have one, don't let that keep you from making this delicious recipe. Microwaves and warming drawers are wonderful keep-it-hot options.

Southern Sideboards (Mississippi)

A three-year-old gave this reaction to her Christmas dinner: "I don't like the turkey, but I like the bread he ate."
—Author Unknown

Oven-Fried Fish Sticks

Kids can make these . . . and they're so good. You'll love them, too.

1 pound cod	Vegetable oil cooking spray
¼ cup cornmeal	⅓ cup low-fat mayonnaise
¼ cup seasoned dry bread	1 teaspoon lemon juice
crumbs	2 tablespoons sweet pickle
½ cup skim milk	relish

Move oven rack to position slightly above middle of oven. Heat oven to 500°. Cut cod into 1x3-inch pieces. Mix cornmeal and bread crumbs together in small dish. Dip fish into milk, then coat with cornmeal-bread crumb mixture. Place in ungreased baking pan. Spray vegetable oil cooking spray over fish. Bake, uncovered, about 10 minutes or until fish flakes easily with a fork.

In a small bowl, mix mayonnaise, lemon juice, and pickle relish. Refrigerate until ready to serve with fish. Serves 4.

Editor's Extra: Greek seasoning can liven this up.

Heart Smart Kids Cookbook (Michigan)

Fish Florentine

A luscious and very easy way to serve bland fish. Give it to the family in a baking dish or to your luncheon guests in ramekins.

1 (12-ounce) package frozen	½ cup sour cream
spinach soufflé	½ cup mayonnaise
1–1½ pounds fish fillets (cod,	¼ cup freshly grated Parmesan
flounder, ocean perch, etc.)	cheese

Defrost spinach soufflé 5–6 hours at room temperature or until soft. Press into a 9-inch pie pan. Cut fillets, and arrange on top of soufflé. Mix together sour cream, mayonnaise, and Parmesan; spread over fish. (Can be prepared in advance, covered, and refrigerated.) Bake in a preheated 350° oven for 30 minutes. Serves 4.

Variation: Divide soufflé, fillets, and sour cream mixture between 4 ramekins. Bake at 350° for about 25 minutes.

The Lymes' Heritage Cookbook (New England)

Crab Cakes

A really nice combination of flavors that brings out the best in crabmeat.

¼ cup minced onion
¼ cup minced green bell
  pepper
1 tablespoon butter
1 pound crabmeat
1 tablespoon Worcestershire
2 tablespoons chopped
  pimento

1 teaspoon hot pepper sauce
½ cup mayonnaise
1 teaspoon salt
2 tablespoons chopped parsley
1 egg, well beaten
Bread crumbs
Cracker meal

Sauté onion and bell pepper in butter until translucent. Add to crab-meat with all other ingredients, except cracker meal. Add enough bread crumbs to make mixture stiff enough to shape into cakes. Coat each cake with cracker meal, and fry over moderate heat in a heavy, well-oiled skillet until browned. Makes 6 generous crab cakes.

Variation: For crab casserole, omit bread crumbs and turn mixture into greased casserole dish. Top with buttered bread crumbs. Bake at 350° for 30–45 minutes or until browned and bubbly.

The Smithfield Cookbook (Virginia)

Salmon Sticks

When you're tired of salmon, these are still a treat. And they are so easy!

2 pounds salmon
1 cup all-purpose flour
¾ cup cornmeal
Garlic salt to taste
Onion salt to taste

Black pepper to taste
Cayenne pepper to taste
Paprika to taste
2 eggs

Cut salmon into sticks about ½ inch thick. Combine flour, cornmeal, and spices to taste (Mrs. Dash is a good substitute for the spices listed). In separate bowl, beat eggs. Dip salmon sticks in eggs, and drain brief-ly. Roll sticks in flour mixture. Fry in deep fat 90 seconds to 2 minutes at 350° or until golden brown. Be careful not to overcook. Serve with tartar sauce.

Sharing Our Best (Alaska)

Crab Cakes

Pan-Seared Tilapia with Chile-Lime Butter

Fish never tasted so zesty!

CHILE-LIME BUTTER:

½ stick unsalted butter, softened
1 tablespoon finely chopped shallots
1 teaspoon finely grated fresh lime zest

2 teaspoons fresh lime juice
1 teaspoon minced serrano chile, including seeds
½ teaspoon salt

Combine butter, shallots, lime zest, lime juice, chile, and salt in a bowl; set aside.

6 (6-ounce) pieces skinless tilapia fillets

½ teaspoon salt
2 tablespoons vegetable oil

Pat fish dry, and sprinkle with salt. Heat oil in 12-inch skillet until just smoking, then sauté 3 fillets, turning just once until golden and cooked through, 4–5 minutes. Repeat with remaining fillets. Top each fillet with a dollop of Chile-Lime Butter. Serves 6.

Savor Summerville (South Carolina)

Creamy Deep-Fried Halibut

Needs no sauce; tastes delicious alone.

1 pound halibut chunks
1½ cups prepared ranch salad dressing

1 cup dehydrated potato flakes
Salt to taste
Oil for frying

Dip halibut into ranch dressing, then roll into potato flakes, and deep-fry until golden brown. Remove halibut from frying pan, drain, and salt to taste. Serves 6.

Just for the Halibut (Alaska)

Beef & Pork

Meatloaf

This classic meatloaf is made even better by using crushed cornflakes instead of bread crumbs. Outstanding!

2 eggs, lightly beaten
2 pounds ground chuck
2 cups crushed cornflakes
¾ cup minced onion
¼ cup minced green bell
  pepper

2 tablespoons soy sauce
2½ teaspoons salt
1 tablespoon mustard
¼ cup milk
1 (10¾-ounce) can cream of
  mushroom soup

Preheat oven to 400°. Lightly mix eggs, meat, crumbs, onion, and bell pepper. Combine with remaining ingredients. The secret is to mix well but lightly. Do not pack. In baking dish, shape meat into oval loaf. Bake at 350° for 50 minutes, or till done. Serves 6–8.

Famous Recipes from Mrs. Wilkes' Boarding House (Georgia)

Stuffed Meatloaf

A delicious presentation: the bacon enhances the flavor, the mozzarella adds texture, and the tomato sauce tops it off beautifully.

1 pound ground chuck
2 eggs
1 cup Italian bread crumbs
½ cup finely chopped onion
Salt and pepper to taste

6 slices bacon
2 or more slices mozzarella
  cheese
1 (8-ounce) can tomato sauce

Mix ground chuck, eggs, bread crumbs, and onion well. On a piece of foil, pat meat mixture out to a rectangle ½ inch thick. Season with salt and pepper. Lay strips of bacon longways on meat. Cover with cheese slices. Starting on short side, roll up meat like a jellyroll. Place in greased baking dish, seam side down. Pour tomato sauce over loaf, and bake at 350° for 45–60 minutes till done. Cut into slices. Serves 4.

Editor's Extra: Sprinkle a little snipped parsley on top.

A Pinch of Rose & A Cup of Charm (Mississippi)

Meatballs and Spaghetti

A very old Italian recipe.

1½ pounds ground chuck
1 cup grated Italian cheese
8 small crackers (soaked in
   water and squeezed)
3 large eggs
2 teaspoons salt
1 teaspoon pepper
2 dashes Tabasco Sauce
1 large bunch green onions,
   chopped

½ cup (or less) olive oil
2 (8-ounce) cans tomato purée
2 pints water
2 large garlic cloves, minced
1 cup finely chopped parsley
1 teaspoon salt
½ teaspoon red pepper
1 teaspoon oregano

Combine first 7 ingredients. Mold into small meatballs, about 1½ inches in diameter. Brown meatballs and onions in olive oil. Remove meat; add tomato purée and water. Add garlic, parsley, and seasonings to taste. Cook 1 hour or until reduced to about half. Add meatballs. Simmer 1 hour. Serve over cooked, drained, and buttered spaghetti. Pass additional cheese. Serves 6–8.

A Cook's Tour of Shreveport (Louisiana)

In family life, love is the oil that eases friction, the cement that binds closer together, and the music that brings harmony.
                    —Eve Burrows

Pizza Burgers

A bed of pasta replaces the bun for these burgers.

1 pound ground beef	**2 tablespoons oil**
1 egg	**1 (15-ounce) can tomato sauce**
½ cup Italian bread crumbs	**½ teaspoon oregano**
Salt and pepper to taste	**6 slices mozzarella cheese**

In a large bowl, combine ground beef, egg, bread crumbs, salt, and pepper. Shape into 6 burgers. Heat a large skillet over medium-high heat. Add oil, and brown burgers on both sides. Remove to a plate, and set aside. Reduce heat, and pour off drippings into a cup (discard fat when cooled). To the skillet, add tomato sauce, a little water rinsed in the can, and oregano. Bring to a boil, stirring well. Reduce heat and simmer. Add burgers, cover, and cook 15 minutes. Just before serving, place a slice of mozzarella cheese on each burger, replace cover, and heat till cheese melts. Serve with cooked fusilli pasta and green beans. Serves 4–6.

Good Things to Eat (Mid-Atlantic)

Pizza by the Yard

French bread is an easy and tasty alternative to pizza dough.

1 loaf French bread	**¼ cup chopped ripe olives**
1 pound ground beef, cooked, drained	**½ teaspoon oregano**
30 slices pepperoni	**½ teaspoon salt**
1 (6-ounce) can tomato paste	**1 (8-ounce) package mozzarella cheese, halved diagonally and sliced**
⅓ cup chopped onion	

Cut bread in half lengthwise; set aside. Combine remaining ingredients, except cheese. Mix well. Spread meat mixture evenly on bread halves, and place on cookie sheet. Bake at 400° for 15 minutes. Place cheese over meat mixture, and bake till cheese melts. Serves 6.

The Great Cookbook (Alabama)

Sunday Supper Snack

So simple and delicious . . . and definitely a crowd-pleaser!

1 pound ground chuck	¼ teaspoon thyme
1 medium onion, chopped	¼ teaspoon oregano
1 clove garlic, crushed	1 (12-count) can biscuits
½ cup barbecue sauce	Several slices sharp processed
½ teaspoon salt	cheese

Brown ground chuck, onion, and garlic together. Add barbecue sauce and seasonings, and simmer until meat is cooked. Meanwhile, press a biscuit into each muffin tin, forming cups. Fill cups with meat mixture, and top with a piece of cheese. Bake at 375° for about 10 minutes, until crust is brown. Serves 6.

Of Pots and Pipkins (Virginia)

Italian Cutlets

Mama Mia, these are really good.

1 pound ground beef	3 slices mozzarella cheese,
Salt and pepper to taste	halved
2 tablespoons chopped parsley	1 (1⅝-ounce) package Lawry's
Flour for dredging	spaghetti sauce mix, prepared
2 eggs, beaten	according to package directions
½ cup bread crumbs	½ cup grated Parmesan cheese
¼ cup vegetable oil	

Combine meat, salt, pepper, and parsley. Shape into 6 cutlets. Dredge cutlets in flour, dip in eggs, and roll in crumbs. Sauté cutlets in oil until brown, and place in a baking dish. Put mozzarella slices on each cutlet, cover with prepared spaghetti sauce, and sprinkle with Parmesan cheese. Bake at 400° for 20–25 minutes.

Flavors (Texas)

The most essential part of my day is a proper dinner.
—Rachael Ray

*Gran's Barbecued
Beef Brisket*

Gran's Barbecued Beef Brisket

This takes planning ahead, but it's so good you won't mind giving it all the time it deserves.

1 (5- to 8-pound) beef brisket	**¼ cup beef bouillon**
¼ cup liquid smoke	**1 tablespoon finely minced**
¼ cup Worcestershire sauce	**garlic**
⅓ cup Italian salad dressing	**1 (16-ounce) bottle of your**
½ teaspoon Kitchen Bouquet	**favorite barbecue sauce, divided**
(browning sauce)	

FIRST DAY:

Remove the fatty membrane from the back of the brisket. Place brisket on a large sheet of foil in a large baking dish. Mix next 6 ingredients with 8 ounces barbecue sauce, and pour over brisket. Let stand 15 minutes. Then seal foil and place in refrigerator overnight.

SECOND DAY:

DO NOT UNWRAP. Bake at 300° for 4 hours. Cool in refrigerator overnight.

THIRD DAY:

Remove meat, and discard fat and foil with juices. Slice brisket across the grain with sharp knife, and pour remaining 8 ounces barbecue sauce over meat. Reheat at 350° for 30 minutes. Serves 8 or more.

Gran's Gems (Mississippi)

One of the very nicest things about life is the way we must regularly stop whatever it is we are doing and devote our attention to eating.

—Luciano Pavarotti

Hamburger Steaks with Mushrooms in Brown Gravy

A repeat-performance favorite and so easy to prepare.

2 pounds lean ground beef	½ onion, chopped
2 eggs	½ cup bread crumbs
½ teaspoon salt	1 tablespoon Worcestershire

Mix all ingredients. Form into 8 steaks. Bake or pan-fry until done to your liking. Save drippings. Remove to a sprayed baking dish.

BROWN GRAVY:

1 (4-ounce) can sliced mushrooms, drained	3 tablespoons cornstarch, mixed with 2 tablespoons warm water
2 cups water	

Place reserved drippings in a pot over medium heat. Add mushrooms and water. When liquid boils, stir in cornstarch mixture until completely incorporated. Remove from heat; pour over steaks in baking dish. Bake at 350° for 10 minutes. Serve with mashed potatoes or rice.

Editor's Extra: Season gravy with salt and pepper or a mixed blend.

Burnt Offerings II (Tennessee)

Poor Man's Steak

This is one of my favorite ways to eat ground beef. My family loves it, too.

1 pound ground beef	Flour
1 teaspoon salt	1 (10¾-ounce) can cream of mushroom soup
1 onion, finely chopped	1 can water
1 cup cracker crumbs	
1 cup milk	

Combine ground beef, salt, onion, cracker crumbs, and milk. Mix well, and pack in loaf pan. Let stand in refrigerator overnight.

Remove from pan, slice, dredge each piece in flour, and brown in greased skillet. Then place in shallow baking pan. Pour soup diluted with water over meat. Bake at 300° for 1½ hours.

Cooking with the Menno Haven Auxiliary (Pennsylvania)

Killer Flank Steak

This is a deliciously different soy sauce marinade.

1 (2-pound) flank steak, trimmed of fat	½ tablespoon dried Italian seasoning
¼ cup soy sauce	1 tablespoon lemon juice
¼ cup olive oil	2 garlic cloves, minced

Place steak in a covered container or zipper bag. Combine remaining ingredients, and pour over steak. Marinate at least 20 minutes at room temperature, or up to 24 hours in the refrigerator, turning occasionally.

Grill over medium coals for 6 minutes. Turn, and grill for an additional 6–8 minutes or until cooked to desired doneness. Slice thinly on the diagonal. Serves 4.

Gold'n Delicious (Washington)

Beef Stroganoff

This stretches a pound of meat deliciously.

1 cup chopped onion	Salt and pepper to taste
2 garlic cloves, chopped	1 package dry onion soup mix
2 cups chopped fresh mushrooms, or 2 (8-ounce) cans sliced mushrooms	¼ cup water
	2 (10¾-ounce) cans cream of mushroom soup
3 tablespoons butter or margarine, divided	½ cup ketchup
1 pound sirloin or round steak	1 pint sour cream
	Cooked noodles or rice

Brown onion, garlic, and mushrooms in 2 tablespoons butter or margarine. Remove from pan, and set aside. Add 1 tablespoon butter or margarine to pan. Cut beef into very thin strips. Brown well; season to taste. Add onion soup mix to the meat; add water. Mix in mushroom soup and onion mixture, and simmer 1 hour, then add ketchup. Stir in sour cream just before ready to serve. Serve over cooked noodles or rice. Serves 6–8.

Dude Food (Utah)

Swiss Steak

This is cooking like our parents and grandparents taught us. It smells so good cooking, looks like you can't wait to dive in, and the taste lives up to the expectations.

½ cup flour
1 teaspoon salt
¼ teaspoon pepper
2 pounds round or cube steak

⅓ cup vegetable oil
1 onion, sliced
1 carrot, sliced

Mix flour, salt and pepper together. Dredge steak in flour mixture (save flour), and brown lightly in a skillet in hot fat or oil, 2 minutes on each side. Reserve oil in skillet. Place meat in baking pan. Top with onion and carrot. Cover with Swiss Steak Gravy, and bake until tender (1 hour) in 350° oven. Serves 6.

SWISS STEAK GRAVY:
2 tablespoons flour
1 teaspoon salt
¼ teaspoon pepper
2 tablespoons reserved oil or
   butter

½ cup tomato juice
2½ cups beef stock or warm water
Few drops Kitchen Bouquet

Stir flour, salt, and pepper in reserved oil over medium heat until flour is lightly brown. Add remaining ingredients, stirring constantly until thickened.

Recipes of the Durbin (Indiana)

Family faces are like magic mirrors. Looking at people who belong to us, we see the past, present, and future.

—Gail Lumet Buckley

Swiss Steak

Chicken Fried Steak
and Cream Gravy

Keep with tradition by serving with hot biscuits topped with the gravy.

2 pounds boneless round steak	½ teaspoon garlic salt
1 cup all-purpose flour	2 eggs
1 teaspoon salt	¼ cup milk
1 teaspoon pepper	Vegetable oil

Trim excess fat from steak; pound steak to ¼-inch thickness, using a meat mallet or the side of saucer. Cut into serving-size pieces. Combine flour, salt, pepper, and garlic salt. Combine eggs and milk; beat well. Dredge steak in flour mixture, dip in egg mixture, then dredge in flour mixture again. Lightly pound steak again. Heat 1 inch of oil in a skillet to 375°. Fry steak in hot oil until browned, turning steak once. Drain on paper towels. Reserve ¼ cup pan drippings for Cream Gravy. Serve steak topped with Cream Gravy. Serves 6–8.

CREAM GRAVY:

¼ cup all-purpose flour	½ teaspoon salt
¼ cup pan drippings	¼ teaspoon pepper
2–3 cups milk	

Add flour to pan drippings; cook over medium heat until bubbly, stirring constantly. Gradually add milk; cook until thickened and bubbly, stirring constantly. Stir in salt and pepper.

Golden Moments (Mississippi)

Sitting down for dinner not only helps you learn, but also teaches you how to listen— which I feel is the most important skill to have.
—Michael Symon

Beef Parmesan

This freezable, pleasable dish is guaranteed to become a family favorite—no doubt about it.

1½ pounds round steak
½ cup grated Parmesan cheese
½ cup bread crumbs
2 eggs, beaten
⅓ cup vegetable oil
1 medium-size onion, chopped
1 teaspoon salt
¼ teaspoon black pepper

1 teaspoon sugar
½ teaspoon marjoram
3 garlic cloves, or to taste
1 (6-ounce) can tomato paste
1 cup hot water
1 (8-ounce) package mozzarella
   cheese slices
Cooked buttered noodles

Place meat between 2 pieces of wax paper; lay on cutting board and pound thin. Cut into thin, small, bite-size pieces. Mix Parmesan cheese and bread crumbs. Dip meat in beaten eggs, then roll in bread crumbs.

Heat oil in skillet, and brown steak. Place in 3-quart baking dish. In same skillet, cook onion until soft. Stir in seasonings, garlic, and tomato paste. Add hot water, and stir. Pour part of sauce over meat; top with cheese slices, and add remaining sauce. Bake at 350° for 1 hour. Serve over cooked buttered noodles. Serves 6 or more.

Note: Great to prepare in advance and freeze. If you plan to freeze it, cook for 45 minutes instead of 1 hour, then freeze. When ready to serve, thaw, and cook about 30 minutes at 350°.

Sand in My Shoes (Florida)

There is no doubt that it is around the family and the home that all the greatest virtues, the most dominating virtues of human, are created, strengthened, and maintained.
—Winston Churchill

Bar-B-Que Beef

This is one of my family's favorites. It is full of flavor and quite addictive!

1 (5- to 6-pound) rump roast	¼ cup brown sugar
2½ tablespoons liquid smoke, divided	1 tablespoon Worcestershire
	½ teaspoon salt
1 (28- to 32-ounce) bottle ketchup	1 teaspoon garlic salt (optional)
	½ teaspoon Tabasco Sauce

Rub roast on all sides with 2 tablespoons liquid smoke. Wrap in foil, and bake in shallow baking dish at 325° for 20–30 minutes per pound. Cool, and slice as thinly as possible. Return to foil. Mix remaining ingredients to make sauce, and pour over sliced meat. Close foil, and let meat stand overnight in refrigerator. Reheat at 275° for 1 hour in foil package.

Vaer saa god Cookbook (Minnesota)

Crockpot Roast

Love this roast! Very easy to make and full of flavor!

1 onion, chopped	½ teaspoon dry rosemary
2 garlic cloves, minced	½ teaspoon dry thyme
1 (4-pound) rump roast	¾ cup red wine (or beef broth)
2 teaspoons salt	3 tablespoons all-purpose flour
¼ teaspoon pepper	¼ cup water

Put onion and garlic in crockpot, and set roast on top. Sprinkle with salt, pepper, rosemary, and thyme. Pour in the wine. Cover, and cook on HIGH setting about 5 hours, until meat is very tender. Remove roast to a serving plate. Measure 2 cups of the cooking liquid into a sauce-pan. Stir together flour and water, and whisk into liquid. Bring to a boil, stirring. Reduce heat, and simmer 10 minutes. Slice the roast, and serve with the gravy. Serves 8–10.

Our Lady of Mercy Church Recipes (New York)

Cola Roast

This is about as easy as it gets, and just as tasty!

1 (3-pound) beef roast
1 envelope dry onion soup mix

2 (12-ounce) cans cola (diet cola
   cannot be substituted)

Place roast in greased 4- to 5-quart slow cooker. Sprinkle with soup mix. Pour cola over all. Cover, and cook on LOW heat 7–8 hours. Serves 4–6.

101 Things To Do With a Slow Cooker (Utah)

Grandma's Pot Roast

This recipe takes me back to my grandma's house . . . Sunday dinners and fond memories.

1 (3- to 4-pound) beef chuck
   roast
2 garlic cloves, minced
Salt and pepper to taste
Oil
1 cup water
1 bay leaf

2 medium onions, cut into
   wedges
8 potatoes, cut into wedges
2 stalks celery, cut into 2-inch
   pieces
6 carrots, cut into 2-inch pieces

Rub outside of roast with garlic, and season with salt and pepper. Brown roast in large frying pan with a small amount of oil until well browned. Place in roasting pan. Add water and bay leaf to frying pan that the meat was browned in, and cook until water boils. Pour water into roasting pan. Cover, and roast at 325° for 35–40 minutes. Place onions, potatoes, celery, and carrots around the meat and cook until vegetables are done. Use drippings from meat, and thicken with flour and water to make gravy. Spoon gravy over meat and vegetables.

Favorite Utah Pioneer Recipes (Utah)

*S*trange to see how a good dinner and feasting reconciles everybody.

—Samuel Pepys

Busy Day Chops

Busy Day Chops

So quick and easy to prepare, you can practically throw it together, put it in the oven, and let the yummy aroma call you to dinner.

¼ cup butter
1 cup rice, uncooked
1 (10½-ounce) can beef broth

1 (10½-ounce) can French
   onion soup
4–6 pork chops

Melt butter in frying pan; add rice, and stir constantly over low heat till brown. Transfer to a 2½-quart casserole dish; add broth and soup, and top with pork chops. Cover, and bake at 350° for 1½ hours. Pork chops will be tender and flavorful! Serves 4–6.

Note: For variety, add chopped bell pepper, celery, and mushrooms.

Editor's Extra: Brown the salt and peppered pork chops before baking. Looks and tastes even better.

Stir Crazy! (South Carolina)

Harvest Pork Chops

This is nice served with baked squash or corn.

6 loin or rib pork chops, cut
   ¾ inch thick
¼ cup flour
½ teaspoon salt
Dash of pepper

3 orange slices, cut in half
3 lemon slices, cut in half
2 tablespoons brown sugar
½ cup orange juice
¼ cup water

Trim all fat from chops; mix flour, salt, and pepper, and rub well into both sides of chops. Heat a large heavy frying pan with ovenproof handle. Brown chops on both sides in small amount of hot fat. Pour off fat.

Place an orange half slice and lemon half slice on each chop. Sprinkle with brown sugar. Mix orange juice and water; pour over and around chops. Bake at 325° for 40–50 minutes, or until chops are tender when tested with a fork. Serve on a hot platter, and garnish with more lemon and orange slices and parsley, if desired.

Cooking with Kiwanis (New Mexico)

Clinton County Pork Chops with Sour Cream Sauce

Very simple, fairly quick, and the results are delicious!

6 loin pork chops
¾ cup water, divided
2 tablespoons brown sugar
2 tablespoons finely chopped
  onion
2 tablespoons ketchup

1 garlic clove, minced
1 beef bouillon cube, or
  1 teaspoon instant beef
  bouillon
2 tablespoons flour
½ cup sour cream

In a large skillet, brown pork chops. Add ½ cup water, brown sugar, onion, ketchup, garlic, and bouillon cube. Cover, and simmer 30–40 minutes, until tender. Remove chops to serving platter; keep warm.

In a small bowl, combine flour with remaining ¼ cup water. Slowly add to cooking liquid, stirring constantly. Stir in sour cream; heat thoroughly. Do not boil. Serve sauce over chops. Serves 6.

Remembering the Past—Planning for the Future (Missouri)

Citrus Spareribs

A rib lover's delight. Tangy, tender, and flavorful.

4–5 pounds spareribs, cut in
  serving pieces
½ (12-ounce) can frozen
  orange juice concentrate,
  thawed, undiluted
¾ cup ketchup

2 tablespoons molasses
1 teaspoon Worcestershire
½ teaspoon Tabasco Sauce
2 teaspoons salt
4 teaspoons grated onion

Place spareribs in large pot. Cover with water, and bring to a boil. Reduce heat, and simmer, covered, for 30 minutes. Drain, and refrigerate until ready to grill.

Mix orange juice concentrate with remaining ingredients. Place spareribs on grill set about 8 inches from heat. Cook 15 minutes. Turn and brush with orange sauce. Cook 15–30 minutes longer, turning and brushing frequently with sauce. Serves 4–6.

Citrus Lovers Cook Book (Florida)

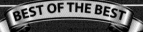
Cakes

Butterscotch Heavenly Delight

This cake is as good as it sounds! This rich and satisfying cake with a surprising toffee crunch is great as a party cake for a special celebration, or as a wonderful way to end a meal.

1 (9½-inch) angel food cake	5½ ounces butterscotch
¾ pound English toffee	topping
1½ cups whipping cream	½ teaspoon vanilla extract

Prepare angel food cake from scratch or package mix. Let cake cool. Slice horizontally into 3 layers. In food processor, with the largest blade, crush toffee using pulse setting. Set aside. Using electric mixer, whip cream until it starts to thicken. Slowly add butterscotch topping and vanilla, and continue beating until thick. Fold all but ¼ cup crushed toffee into whipped cream mixture.

Place bottom layer of angel food cake on a cake plate, and spread butterscotch mixture over top. Repeat with second layer, then third, frosting sides as well. Sprinkle reserved ¼ cup crushed toffee over top of cake. Refrigerate for a minimum of 6 hours. Serves 12.

Editor's Extra: You can use a store-bought angel food cake, and packaged toffee bits can sub for the English toffee.

LaConner Palates (Washington)

What greater thing is there for human souls than to feel that they are joined for life—to be with each other in silent unspeakable memories.

—George Eliot

Angel Berry Tunnel Cake

A happy dessert for calorie counters. So pretty when sliced to serve.

1 (10-inch) prepared angel food cake	1½ cups fresh or frozen blueberries
1½ cups frozen raspberries or strawberries, thawed and drained	1 (8-cup) carton whipped topping Additional berries for garnish

With a serrated knife, slice off top ½ inch of cake. Set aside. Cut a tunnel ring about 2 inches deep in the cake, leaving a ¾-inch shell. Remove cake from tunnel. Cut into 1-inch cubes. Combine cake cubes, berries, and ½ of whipped topping. Spoon into tunnel. Replace cake top. Frost with remaining whipped topping. Garnish with berries, if desired. Refrigerate until serving. Serves 12.

Note: May use sliced fresh raspberries or strawberries.

Iuka Masonic Lodge Cookbook (Mississippi)

7-UP Cake

An old favorite that stands the test of time.

1 (18¼-ounce) box lemon cake mix	½ cup cooking oil
1 (3-ounce) box instant lemon pudding mix	4 eggs 10 ounces 7-UP
1 (8-ounce) can crushed pineapple, drained	7 teaspoons lemon juice ¾–1 cup powdered sugar

Combine all ingredients, except lemon juice and powdered sugar. Bake in 9x13-inch pan at 350° for 40–45 minutes.

Combine lemon juice and powdered sugar; mix well, and pour over hot cake.

Editor's Extra: You can use Sprite or any other lemon-lime soda. And a yellow cake mix can sub for the lemon cake mix, as well.

Taste & See (Indiana)

Banana-Pineapple Upside-Down Cake

A true Hawaiian treat!

BATTER:

⅜ cup (6 tablespoons) butter, softened
¾ cup sugar
1 egg, beaten
2 cups all-purpose flour
2 teaspoons baking powder
½ teaspoon salt
¾ cup milk
1 banana, mashed

Preheat oven to 350°. Cream butter with sugar; add beaten egg. Sift flour, baking powder, and salt; add gradually with milk to butter mixture. Fold in banana.

TOPPING:

⅓ cup (5½ tablespoons) butter
⅔ cup brown sugar
½ cup chopped nuts
1 cup crushed pineapple, well drained

Melt butter in 9-inch square pan or small tube pan. Sprinkle brown sugar over butter; then add nuts and pineapple to pan. Pour Batter over Topping, and bake 25–30 minutes. Serves 6–8.

Cook 'em Up Kaua'i (Hawaii)

There's nothing that makes you more insane than family. Or more happy. Or more exasperated. Or more . . . secure.
—Jim Butcher, *Vignette*

Banana-Pineapple Upside-Down Cake

Banana Cake

To say this is the best banana cake in the world would be an understatement.

2 small bananas	2 eggs
1 teaspoon lemon juice	½ cup milk
2 cups sugar	1½ teaspoons baking soda
2 sticks butter, softened	2 cups all-purpose flour

Grease 2 large cake pans, and line with wax paper rounds that you have cut to fit. Mash bananas, and add lemon juice to prevent browning. Cream together sugar, butter, and eggs. Add milk and baking soda, alternating with flour. Mix in bananas. Bake at 350° for about 30 minutes. Cool.

FROSTING:

1 (8-ounce) package cream cheese, softened	1 (1-pound) box powdered sugar
½ stick butter, softened	1 teaspoon vanilla
	Chopped nuts

Combine cream cheese, butter, powdered sugar, and vanilla. Spread on cooled cake layers, and sprinkle top layer with chopped nuts.

Village Royale: Our Favorite Recipes (Florida)

Poppy Seed Cake

Nice to slice these loaves and take to occasions. Slices go easily into lunch boxes.

1 (18¼-ounce) box white cake mix	4 eggs
1 (3-ounce) package instant coconut pudding mix	¼ cup poppy seeds
	½ cup oil
	1 cup hot water

Beat all ingredients with electric mixer 4 minutes. Pour into 2 greased loaf pans. Bake at 350° for 40 minutes. Serves 8–12.

Variation: Substitute lemon cake mix or lemon instant pudding mix.

Editor's Extra: If coconut pudding cannot be found, use French vanilla and add 2 teaspoons coconut extract.

Visitation Parish Cookbook (Iowa)

Gram's Chocolate Cake

A big sheet pan full of chocolate-iced squares.

2 cups all-purpose flour	1 teaspoon baking soda
2 cups sugar	1 teaspoon vanilla
2 sticks butter	½ cup buttermilk
4 tablespoons cocoa	2 eggs
1 cup water	

Combine flour and sugar in bowl. In saucepan, heat butter, cocoa, and water until melted. Pour over flour and sugar; mix to combine. Add baking soda, vanilla, buttermilk, and eggs; beat well. Bake on greased and floured jellyroll pan at 350° for 15–20 minutes. Frost while warm.

GRAM'S CHOCOLATE FROSTING:

1 stick butter, softened	1 teaspoon vanilla
4 tablespoons cocoa	2 cups powdered sugar
6 tablespoons milk	

Combine all ingredients; beat well.

Family Favorites from the Heart (Utah)

Nashville's One-Pan Fudge Cake

So easy and so fudgy good.

½ cup butter, melted	¼ teaspoon baking powder
1¼ ounces bittersweet chocolate, melted	2 eggs
	1 teaspoon vanilla
1 cup sugar	1 cup broken nuts
½ cup all-purpose flour	⅛ teaspoon salt

Combine melted butter, chocolate, and sugar in medium bowl. Sift flour and baking powder into same bowl. Add eggs, vanilla, nuts, and salt. Blend, and pour into a well-greased 8-inch square pan. Bake at 325° for 35 minutes. Cut into squares while hot, but do not remove from pan till cooled. Makes 1 dozen squares.

Nashville Seasons (Tennessee)

Peanut Butter Sheet Cake

If you like peanut butter, you'll LOVE this cake.

½ cup peanut butter	2 cups all-purpose flour
½ cup oil	½ cup milk
1 stick butter or margarine	2 eggs, beaten
1 cup water	1 teaspoon baking soda
2 cups sugar	1 teaspoon vanilla

Boil together peanut butter, oil, butter, and water. Remove from heat; add sugar, flour, milk, eggs, baking soda, and vanilla. (This is a very thin batter.) Pour into greased 9x13-inch pan, and bake 20–25 minutes in 375° oven.

PEANUT BUTTER FROSTING:

½ cup peanut butter	1 pound powdered sugar
⅓ cup milk	1 teaspoon vanilla
1 stick butter or margarine	

Boil together the peanut butter, milk, and butter. Remove from heat, and add powdered sugar and vanilla. Beat until smooth, and spread on cake that has cooled slightly.

Cakes . . . Cakes . . . and more Cakes (West Virginia)

That's what people do who love you. They put their arms around you and love you when you're not so lovable.
—Deb Caletti

Carrot Cake

The crushed pineapple makes this cake extra moist. Everyone asks for the recipe.

2 cups all-purpose flour	1½ cups oil
2 teaspoons baking powder	4 eggs
1½ teaspoons baking soda	2 cups grated carrots
2 teaspoons cinnamon	1 (8-ounce) can crushed
1 teaspoon salt	pineapple, drained
2 cups sugar	½ cup chopped nuts

Sift flour, baking powder, baking soda, cinnamon, and salt. Cream sugar and oil. Add eggs, beating after each addition. Stir in sifted ingredients, carrots, pineapple, and nuts. Bake in 3 (8- or 9-inch) greased and floured pans in 350° oven for 35–40 minutes. Cool before icing.

CREAM CHEESE ICING:

1 (1-pound) box powdered	1 teaspoon vanilla
sugar	1 (8-ounce) package cream
1 stick butter or margarine,	cheese, softened
softened	

Combine ingredients, and beat till smooth. Icing may be tinted with a few drops of green food coloring.

Heart of the Home Recipes (Great Plains)

When one door of happiness closes, another opens; but often we look so long at the closed door that we do not see the one which has been opened for us.
      —Helen Keller

Fresh Strawberry Cake

Pretty layers of goodness that make you want to dive in head first. But don't . . . you'll want to savor every bite.

1 (18¼-ounce) box yellow
   cake mix
1 (8-ounce) package cream
   cheese, softened
½ cup powdered sugar

½ cup sugar
1 (16-ounce) carton Cool Whip
2 cartons fresh strawberries,
   sliced thin
1 jar strawberry glaze

Bake cake according to package directions for 2 cake pans; allow to cool. Cool; then cut the layers with a piece of thread to make 4 layers. Mix cream cheese and sugars together. Fold in Cool Whip. In another bowl, mix sliced strawberries and glaze together. Start with one layer of cake; spread with a layer of cream cheese mixture, then a layer of strawberry glaze mixture. Repeat with each layer. Keep in refrigerator.

Recipes & Remembrances (Alabama)

Fresh Apple Cake

1¼ cups vegetable oil
2 cups sugar
3 cups all-purpose flour
1 teaspoon salt
1 teaspoon baking soda

3 eggs
2 teaspoons vanilla
2 cups chopped apples
1 cup chopped nuts
1 cup flaked coconut

Combine oil and sugar; add dry ingredients alternately with eggs, beating after each addition. Add vanilla, chopped apples, nuts, and coconut. Spoon into greased tube pan. Bake 1 hour and 15 minutes at 350°.

TOPPING:
1 cup sugar
¼ cup milk

1 stick butter, melted

Combine ingredients, and drizzle on warm cake.

Miss Patti's Cook Book (Kentucky)

Fresh Strawberry Cake

A Good Cake

Is certainly is!

1 (18¼-ounce) box spice cake mix	1 cup water
1 (3-ounce) box butterscotch instant pudding mix	½ cup strawberry preserves
¾ cup oil	½ cup raisins
4 eggs	1 cup canned flaked coconut
	1 cup chopped pecans

Preheat oven to 325°. Combine cake mix and pudding mix. Add oil, eggs, water, and preserves, beating with each addition; beat well. Add raisins, coconut, and pecans; mix till well blended. Pour into a well-greased Bundt pan; bake 1 hour. Leave in pan to cool. Serves 16.

SAUCE: (OPTIONAL)

1 cup powdered sugar	Juice of 1½ lemons

Mix powdered sugar and lemon juice. After cooling cake about 10 minutes, punch holes in cake with a fork. Pour Sauce over cake, letting it soak in while continuing to cool.

Dixie Dining (Mississippi)

Perhaps the greatest social service that can be rendered by anybody to this country and to mankind is to bring up a family.
—George Bernard Shaw

Lemon Cake

Lemonylicious.

1 (3-ounce) box lemon Jell-O	¾ cup oil
1 cup hot water	4 eggs
1 (18¼-ounce) box lemon	1 cup powdered sugar
cake mix	1½ teaspoons lemon juice

Dissolve Jell-O in hot water until clear. Mix cake mix, oil, and Jell-O mixture together. Add eggs, 1 at a time. Pour into lightly greased 9x13-inch baking dish. Bake in a 350° oven for 30–35 minutes till done. While still hot, prick with fork. Mix powdered sugar with lemon juice to make light glaze. Glaze while cake is hot.

Our Best Home Cooking (West Virginia)

Buttermilk Pound Cake

Moistened by a buttery, lemony, saucy glaze. Yum.

1 cup butter, softened	3 cups all-purpose flour
2 cups sugar	⅛ teaspoon salt
4 eggs	½ teaspoon baking soda
1–2 teaspoons lemon flavoring	1 cup buttermilk

Cream butter; add sugar gradually, and cream well. Add eggs, one at a time, beating well after each addition. Add lemon flavoring, and mix well. Combine flour, salt, and baking soda; add to sugar mixture alternately with buttermilk. Bake in lightly greased tube pan at 325° for 1–1¼ hours. Cool, and invert out of pan.

GLAZE:

¼ cup butter	¼ cup lemon juice
⅔ cup sugar	

Melt butter and sugar till sugar is dissolved; add lemon juice. Allow cake to thoroughly cool before glazing.

Editor's Extra: I poke some holes in the top before glazing to let some of the Glaze flavor the inside as well.

Mountain Recipe Collection (Kentucky)

Caramel Pound Cake

CAKE:

2 sticks butter or margarine, softened
½ cup Crisco
3 cups sugar
6 eggs

4 cups all-purpose flour
½ teaspoon baking powder
1 cup milk
1 teaspoon vanilla

In a large bowl, cream together butter, Crisco, and sugar. Add eggs, one at a time, to creamed butter mixture. In another bowl, mix flour and baking powder, then add to creamed butter mixture. Add milk and vanilla; mix well. Bake at 300° in a well-greased and floured tube pan for 1½ hours, longer, if cake doesn't spring back to touch. Cool.

CARAMEL ICING:

1 stick butter or margarine
1 cup brown sugar
¼ cup milk

2 cups powdered sugar
½ teaspoon vanilla

In a saucepan, melt butter and brown sugar. Let bubble; stir. Add milk. Remove from heat, add powdered sugar, and beat with an electric mixer. Add vanilla, mix well, and spread on cooled cake.

A Taste Through Time (South Carolina)

A woman is like a tea bag; you never know how strong it is until it's in hot water.
—Eleanor Roosevelt

Granny's Blueberry Pound Cake

A summer treat! This delicious cake is nice to take on picnics since it is easy to wrap and pack.

2 sticks butter or margarine,
    softened
2 cups sugar
4 eggs
1½ teaspoons vanilla

1 pint blueberries, washed
    and drained well
3 cups all-purpose flour, divided
1 teaspoon baking powder
½ teaspoon salt

Preheat oven to 325°. Grease and flour a 10-inch tube pan. Use electric mixer to cream butter and sugar. Add eggs, one at a time, beating well after each egg is added. Add vanilla, and beat until fluffy.

Dredge berries in ¼ cup flour, and set aside. Sift remaining 2¾ cups flour with baking powder and salt; fold into cake batter until well blended. Gently stir in berries. Pour into pan, and bake about 1 hour and 10 minutes or until cake tester, inserted near center, comes out clean. Place on rack, and cool 10 minutes before removing from pan. Serves 12–16.

Note: Well-drained frozen or canned berries can be used.

Words Worth Eating (Virginia)

You can kiss your family and friends goodbye and put miles between you, but at the same time you carry them with you in your heart, your mind, your stomach, because you do not just live in a world, but a world lives in you.
            —Frederick Buechner

Key Lime Cheesecake

Tastes just like Cheesecake Factory's. And that's outstanding!

CRUST:

1¾ cups graham cracker crumbs

5 tablespoons butter, melted

1 tablespoon sugar

Combine crumbs, butter, and sugar in a bowl. Stir well to coat crumbs, keeping crumbly. Press crumbs into bottom and halfway up the side of an 8-inch springform pan. Bake at 350° for 5 minutes, and set aside.

FILLING:

3 (8-ounce) packages cream cheese, softened

1 cup sugar

1 teaspoon vanilla extract

½ cup fresh lime juice (about 5 limes)

3 eggs

Whipped cream

In a large bowl, combine cream cheese, sugar, and vanilla. Beat with electric mixer until smooth. Add lime juice and eggs, and continue to beat until smooth and creamy. Pour Filling into Crust. Bake 60–70 minutes at 350° in a water bath. When top turns light brown, it is done. Remove from oven, and allow to cool at room temperature.

With a knife, loosen edges around springform pan. Refrigerate. When chilled, remove pan sides. Slice, and serve with whipped cream.

Editor's Extra: I wrap the springform pan all the way up the sides with tin foil to be sure the water bath doesn't leak in or the cake out! A water bath is when you put the cake pan into a larger pan of water—it should come halfway up the sides. It's a French thing—bain-marie means to heat gently and gradually to fixed temperatures.

Delightfully Seasoned Recipes (Virginia)

A golfer's diet: Live on greens as much as possible.

—Author Unknown

Key Lime Cheesecake

Butterscotch Cheesecake

⅓ cup butter, melted
1½ cups graham cracker
  crumbs
⅓ cup firmly packed brown
  sugar
1 (14-ounce) can sweetened
  condensed milk (not
  evaporated)
¾ cup cold water

1 (3⅝-ounce) package
  butterscotch pudding mix
3 (8-ounce) packages cream
  cheese, softened
3 eggs
1 teaspoon vanilla extract
Whipped cream
Crushed hard butterscotch candy

Preheat oven to 375°. Combine butter, crumbs, and sugar; press firmly on bottom of 9-inch springform pan.

In medium saucepan, combine sweetened condensed milk and water; mix well. Stir in pudding mix. Over medium heat, cook and stir until thickened and bubbly.

In a large mixing bowl, beat cream cheese until fluffy. Beat in eggs and vanilla, then pudding mixture. Pour into prepared pan. Bake 50 minutes or until golden brown around edge (center will be soft). Cool to room temperature. Chill thoroughly. Garnish with whipped cream and crushed candy. Refrigerate leftovers.

The Stirling City Hotel Favorite Recipes (California)

*D*inner Conversation Starters:

- *What language would you most like to speak fluently?*

- *What place and in what time period would you like to visit for a day?*

- *Would would you buy first if you suddenly were given a million dollars and had to spend it in one day?*

Cookies & Candies

Chewy Chocolate Oatmeal Cookies

The only thing that would make these better is a glass of cold milk.

½ cup Hershey's cocoa
½ cup butter or margarine,
  melted
1 (14-ounce) can sweetened
  condensed milk
2 eggs, beaten
2 teaspoons vanilla

1½ cups quick-cooking
  oatmeal
1 cup biscuit baking mix
¼ teaspoon salt
1 (12-ounce) package Hershey's
  vanilla milk chips (or peanut
  butter chips)

Preheat oven to 350°. In large bowl, combine cocoa and melted butter until smooth. Stir in remaining ingredients until well blended. Let dough stand 10 minutes. Drop by heaping teaspoonfuls onto lightly greased cookie sheet. Bake 7–9 minutes; remove from baking sheets. Cool completely. Store tightly covered.

Winniehaha's Favorite Recipes (Minnesota)

Texas Ranger Cookies

A good treat after a long day on the range.

1 stick butter or margarine,
  softened
½ cup shortening
1 cup sugar
1 cup brown sugar
2 eggs
2 cups all-purpose flour
1 teaspoons baking soda

½ teaspoon baking powder
½ teaspoon salt
1 teaspoon vanilla
2 cups quick-cooking oatmeal
2 cups Rice Krispies
1 cup chopped pecans
1 cup flaked coconut

Cream together butter, shortening, sugars, and eggs. Sift together flour, baking soda, baking powder, and salt. Gradually add to creamed mixture. Add vanilla. Stir in oats, Rice Krispies, pecans, and coconut. Roll dough into small balls, and flatten on cookie sheet. Bake in a preheated 375° oven for 8 minutes.

The Authorized Texas Ranger Cookbook (Texas)

Chocolate Chunk Pecan Cookies

Imagine dipping these cookies in some milk . . . oh my goodness!

1 stick sweet butter, softened
½ cup white sugar
½ cup dark brown sugar
1 large egg
1 teaspoon vanilla extract
1 cup plus 2 tablespoons
  all-purpose flour
½ teaspoon kosher salt
½ teaspoon baking soda
½ cup chopped pecans
6 ounces good-quality
  bittersweet or semisweet
  chocolate, chopped coarsely

Preheat oven to 375°. With electric mixer, beat butter until creamy. Add sugars, and beat until light and fluffy. Add egg and vanilla, and beat well to combine. Sift together dry ingredients, and add to batter, mixing well. Stir in nuts and chocolate chunks by hand. Drop by teaspoonfuls onto greased cookie sheets, and bake 8–10 minutes until lightly browned. Cool 5 minutes on sheets, then remove cookies with a spatula to racks to cool.

Editor's Extra: Try letting cookies cool on a cut brown paper bag. It absorbs some the oil from the bottom of the cookies.

Never Trust a Skinny Chef...II (Nevada)

White Chocolate and Macadamia Cookies

If you think the name sounds good—wait till you take a bite!

1 stick butter, softened
4 ounces cream cheese,
  softened
½ cup brown sugar
½ cup sugar
1 egg
2 teaspoons vanilla
2 cups all-purpose flour
1 teaspoon baking soda
½ teaspoon salt
1 cup white chocolate morsels
½ cup macadamia nuts

Cream butter, cream cheese, and sugars. Beat in egg and vanilla. Add dry ingredients, and mix on low speed just until combined. Do not overmix. Drop by tablespoonfuls onto cookie sheet. Bake at 300° for 18–20 minutes.

Breaking Bread Together (Mississippi)

Peanut Butter-Kiss Cookies

Peanut Butter-Kiss Cookies

You'll likely get kisses when you make these kisses. This simple mixture will bring raves in minutes.

1 (18¼-ounce) yellow cake mix
2 eggs
⅓ cup oil

¾ cup peanut butter
1 package Hershey's Kisses

Preheat oven to 350°. Combine cake mix, eggs, and oil until mixture reaches brownie consistency. Mix peanut butter into the dough. Drop by heaping teaspoonfuls onto a lightly greased pan. Place an unwrapped chocolate kiss in the center of each dough ball. Bake 10 minutes, or until light golden brown. Remove from pan and cool.

101 Things To Do With a Cake Mix (Utah)

Pumpkin Harvest Cookies

These smell heavenly.

1 cup pumpkin
2 sticks butter or margarine,
  softened
1½ cups brown sugar
2 eggs

2½ cups self-rising flour
1 teaspoon pumpkin pie spice
10 ounces white chocolate,
  chopped
1 cup chopped pecans

Blend pumpkin, butter, brown sugar, and eggs. Combine flour and pumpkin pie spice. Add flour mixture to pumpkin mixture. Add white chocolate and pecans. Chill. Drop by teaspoonfuls onto baking sheet. Bake at 350° for 20 minutes. Makes 100 or so.

Editor's Extra: Cookies should sit on baking pans a couple of minutes after taking from oven. Transfer to racks or brown paper to cool. Cookies bake well on parchment paper-lined cookie sheets; just slide paper off onto counter to cool.

Heavenly Recipes (Kentucky)

Traveling in the company of those we love is home in motion.
—Leigh Hunt

Savannah Cheesecake Cookies

These are a favorite among Savannahians.

CRUST:

1 cup all-purpose flour
½ cup packed light brown
  sugar

1 cup chopped pecans
½ cup (1 stick) butter, melted

Preheat oven to 350°. Combine flour, brown sugar, pecans, and melted butter in a bowl. Press dough into ungreased 9x13x2-inch pan. Bake for 12–15 minutes or until lightly browned.

FILLING:

2 (8-ounce) packages cream
  cheese, softened
1 cup granulated sugar
3 eggs

1 teaspoon pure vanilla or
  almond extract
Fresh berries and mint leaves
  for garnish

Beat cream cheese and granulated sugar together in a bowl until smooth, using a handheld electric mixer; add eggs and extract; beat well. Pour over Crust. Bake 20 minutes. Cool completely. Cut into squares before serving. Decorate with berries and mint leaves. Makes 24 squares.

The Lady & Sons Just Desserts (Georgia)

I think cookies are sort of the unsung sweet, you know? They're incredibly popular. But everybody thinks of cakes and pies and fancier desserts before they think cookies. A plate of cookies is a great way to end dinner and really nice to share at the holidays.
—Bobby Flay

Toffee Shortbread

This is just like the toffee shortbread we used to eat at McCormick's in Staunton when we were in college. They made it in pie pans.

SHORTBREAD:

¾ cup butter, softened

¾ cup sugar

2 cups all-purpose flour

Preheat oven to 350°. Cream together softened butter and sugar. Stir in flour till well mixed. Press batter into a 9-inch pan. Bake 25–30 minutes, till edges are golden brown. Let cool.

TOFFEE AND TOPPING:

½ cup butter

½ cup brown sugar

1 (14-ounce) can sweetened
   condensed milk

2 tablespoons light corn syrup

1 teaspoon vanilla extract

16 ounces chocolate chips

Melt butter in heavy saucepan over medium heat. Add brown sugar, condensed milk, and corn syrup; bring to a boil. Cook 5 minutes, stirring constantly. Remove from heat, and stir in vanilla. Pour over cooled Shortbread. Melt chocolate chips in double boiler. Stir till smooth. Pour over cooled Toffee. Cut into squares.

Editor's Extra: Chocolate melts beautifully in the microwave: two minutes on HIGH in a glass measure. Perfect.

The Sun and the Rain & the Appleseed (Virginia)

Some of the most important conversations I've ever had occurred at my family's dinner table.
　　　　　　　　　　　　　　　　—Bob Ehrlich

Triple Treat Cookies

Triple Treat Cookies

These don't last long around my house!

1 cup white sugar	1 teaspoon vanilla
1 cup brown sugar	3 cups all-purpose flour
1 cup butter, softened	2 teaspoons baking soda
1 cup peanut butter	1½ teaspoons salt
2 eggs	1½ cups chocolate chips

Cream sugars with butter and peanut butter. Add eggs and vanilla. Mix in flour that has been mixed with baking soda and salt. Add chocolate chips. Roll dough into balls. Bake on greased cookie sheets about 10 minutes at 350° till browned.

FILLING:

½ cup peanut butter	1 teaspoon vanilla
⅓ cup milk	3 cups powdered sugar

Combine all ingredients, and press between 2 cookies.

Favorite Recipes from the Heart of Amish Country (Ohio)

Ritzee Lemon Cookie

These are always a hit.

28 Ritz Crackers, crushed fine	1 (3-ounce) package lemon
¼ cup brown sugar	pudding mix
¼ cup all-purpose flour	½ cup flaked coconut
¼ cup butter, melted	

Mix cracker crumbs, brown sugar, flour, and butter with fork, and press ½ the mixture into a 8-inch square pan. Cook lemon pudding, using ¼ cup less liquid than called for. Spread into crust. Sprinkle coconut and remaining cracker mixture over pudding. Bake at 350° for 20–30 minutes. Let stand to cool. Cut into squares.

Grannie Annie's Cookin' at the Homestead (Alaska)

Chocolate Walnut Crumb Bars

This is just pure yummy goodness.

CRUMB CRUST:

1 cup (2 sticks) butter, softened   **½ cup sugar**
2 cups all-purpose flour   **¼ teaspoon salt**

Preheat oven to 350°. Beat butter in large mixing bowl until creamy. Add flour, sugar, and salt; mix until crumbly. With floured fingers, press 2 cups crumb mixture into bottom of greased 9x13-inch baking pan; reserve remaining crust mixture. Bake 10–12 minutes until edges are golden brown.

FILLING:

1 (14-ounce) can sweetened   **1 teaspoon vanilla**
** condensed milk**   **1 cup chopped walnuts**
1 (12-ounce) package
** chocolate chips, divided**

Warm sweetened condensed milk and 1½ cups chocolate chips in small, heavy saucepan over low heat, stirring until smooth. Stir in vanilla. Spread chocolate mixture over hot Crumb Crust. Stir walnuts and remaining chocolate chips into reserved crumb mixture; sprinkle over chocolate filling. Bake 25–30 minutes until center is set. Cool in pan on wire rack. Cut with sharp knife into bars. Makes 24–30.

Kailua Cooks (Hawaii)

All you need is love. But a little chocolate now and then doesn't hurt.
—Charles M. Schulz

Tollhouse Brownies

A new twist on an old favorite.

2 (16-ounce) packages
  refrigerated chocolate chip
  cookie dough, softened
2 eggs

½ cup sugar
1 (8-ounce) package cream
  cheese, at room temperature
1 teaspoon vanilla

Grease well a 9x13-inch pan; spread 1 softened package cookie dough in bottom of pan. Mix eggs, sugar, cream cheese, and vanilla well, and pour over dough. Drop pieces of dough from second package over filling. Bake at 350° for 35 minutes. If top is not brown enough, place under broiler for desired browning. Watch carefully. Refrigerate when cooled. Can also be frozen and eaten as an ice cream-type sandwich. Makes 2 dozen.

RSVP (New England)

German Chocolate
Caramel Brownies

These are simply scrumptious.

1 (14-ounce) package caramels,
  unwrapped
1 (5-ounce) can evaporated
  milk, divided
1 (18¼-ounce) box German
  chocolate cake mix

¾ cup butter or margarine,
  melted
1 cup chocolate chips (6 ounces)

Melt caramels and ⅓ cup evaporated milk over low heat. Combine cake mix, melted butter, remaining ⅓ cup evaporated milk, and chocolate chips. Grease a 9x13-inch baking pan. Press ½ of dough in pan; spread with caramel mixture. Top loosely with remaining dough. Bake 30 minutes at 350°.

Home at the Range II (Great Plains)

Cream Cheese Streusel Brownies

Cream Cheese Streusel Brownies

You'll want to take these to your next bring-a-dish gathering . . . if you can get out of the house with them.

¼ cup cold butter or margarine
1 (21½-ounce) package fudge
   brownie mix, divided
1 cup chopped nuts
2 eggs, used separately
¼ cup vegetable oil

¼ cup water
1 (8-ounce) package cream
   cheese, softened
¼ cup sugar
½ teaspoon vanilla

Heat oven to 350°. Grease bottom of 9x13-inch pan. Cut butter into ½ cup dry brownie mix until crumbly; stir in nuts, and set aside. Mix remaining dry brownie mix, 1 egg, oil, and water. Spread in greased pan. Beat together cream cheese, sugar, and vanilla on medium speed until well blended. Blend in remaining egg. Spread over brownie mixture in pan. Sprinkle with reserved brownie mixture. Bake 40 minutes. Cool completely before cutting into squares. Makes 20 squares.

Family Secrets (Mississippi)

Rocky Road Candy

Just plain yummy!

½ stick (¼ cup) butter or
   margarine
½ (12-ounce) package semisweet
   chocolate pieces

3 cups miniature marshmallows
½ cup chopped nuts

In a saucepan, melt butter and chocolate pieces over low heat. Remove from heat; stir in marshmallows and nuts just until coated with chocolate. Spoon onto wax paper or into buttered pan. Chill until set, about 30 minutes. Makes about 24 pieces.

A Century of Mormon Cookery, Volume 1 (Utah)

Mama's Best Peanut Butter Fudge

Two pans of yummy fudge makes enough for a crowd.

3 tablespoons white corn syrup	1 (18-ounce) jar peanut butter
Evaporated milk (about ¾ cup)	1 (16-ounce) jar marshmallow
4 cups sugar	crème
2 sticks butter	1 tablespoon vanilla

Place corn syrup in measuring cup and add enough evaporated milk to make 1 cup. In heavy saucepan, combine milk mixture with sugar and butter, and cook over low heat, stirring constantly to prevent sticking, until mixture reaches soft-ball stage. Stir in peanut butter and marshmallow crème; add vanilla, and mix well. Pour into 2 buttered 9x13-inch pans, and cool before cutting. Makes 4–6 pounds.

Editor's Extra: Soft-ball stage is 234°–240° on a candy thermometer. If a thermometer is not available, use the cold-water test by spooning a few drops of the hot mixture into a cup of very cold water. The mixture will form a soft, flexible ball. If you remove the ball from water, it will flatten like a pancake after a few moments in your hand.

Sun-Sational Southern Cuisine (North Carolina)

Families are like fudge . . . mostly sweet with a few nuts. —Author Unknown

Chocolate Peanut Butter Balls

Kids and grown-ups love these!

3 cups creamy peanut butter
2 pounds confectioners' sugar
3 sticks butter, melted
4 ounces German sweet chocolate

2 cups chocolate chips
 (12 ounces)
1 square paraffin wax

Mix peanut butter, sugar, and butter thoroughly. Form into balls, and freeze. Melt German chocolate, chocolate chips, and paraffin in double boiler. Dip frozen balls in chocolate. Keep refrigerated until serving. Makes 8 dozen.

It's Our Serve (New York)

Tiger Butter

A quick and easy treat.

1 pound white chocolate,
 chopped
¼ cup semisweet chocolate
 chips

⅓ cup crunchy peanut butter
½ cup crispy rice cereal

Line a 9x9-inch pan with wax paper. Combine white chocolate, chocolate chips, and peanut butter in a 2-quart microwave-safe dish, and microwave on LOW for 1 minute. Stir until smooth. Stir in rice cereal, and spread into prepared pan. Let cool completely before cutting into squares.

Red Flannel Town Recipes (Michigan)

The thing about family disasters is that you never have to wait long before the next one puts the previous one into perspective.
—Robert Brault

Butterscotch Drops

These are addictive!

1 (12-ounce) package
  butterscotch chips
2 tablespoons peanut butter
½–1 cup slivered almonds,
  toasted

2 cups cornflakes
½ teaspoon vanilla
Dash of salt

Melt butterscotch in top of double boiler. Add peanut butter; stir well. Add almonds, cornflakes, vanilla, and salt. Drop by teaspoonful onto greased cookie sheet. Chill till firm. Makes 4–6 dozen. May be frozen for 2 weeks.

Stir Crazy! (South Carolina)

Best in the World Peanut Brittle

Oh! So good!

1 cup white corn syrup
2 cups white sugar
½ cup water
2 cups raw peanuts

2 teaspoons butter or margarine
2 teaspoons vanilla
2 teaspoons baking soda
½ teaspoon salt

Butter a large platter well. Place corn syrup, sugar, and water in large iron skillet, and cook to soft-ball stage (234°–240° on a candy thermometer). Add shelled raw peanuts. Stir and cook these ingredients on medium-high heat to crack stage (301°–302°), stirring constantly. Turn off heat. Stir in butter, vanilla, baking soda, and salt until well blended. This will want to foam over. Keep stirring fast until well blended. Pour into prepared platter. As soon as possible, start pulling over the edges of platter. Work on Formica or tile counter. You can't pull this out thin until it reaches the right temperature, when it is clear. (If it's too hot, it will not be clear, so just keep working with it.) You can make it as thin as you like, and break it into pieces.

Peanut Palate Pleasers from Portales (New Mexico)

Pies & Other Desserts

Dutch Peach Pie

A Stonewall, Texas "Peach Jamboree" recipe.

10–12 ripe peaches	**¼ teaspoon salt**
1 (9-inch) unbaked pastry shell	**2 tablespoons flour**
1 egg, slightly beaten	**½ teaspoon cinnamon**
1 cup sour cream	**½ teaspoon nutmeg**
¾ cup sugar	

Preheat oven to 350°. Peel peaches, slice, and arrange in pastry shell. Mix egg with sour cream, sugar, salt, flour, cinnamon and nutmeg. Pour over peaches, and bake 20 minutes.

TOPPING:

2 tablespoons butter	**3 tablespoons flour**
¼ cup brown sugar	**½ cup chopped nuts**

Cut butter into sugar, flour, and chopped nuts; sprinkle over pie, and continue to bake 12–15 minutes.

A Texas Hill Country Cookbook (Texas)

Family life is a bit like a runny peach pie—not perfect, but who's complaining?
—Robert Brault

Bogberry Apple Tart

Great warm with ice cream! (And cold will be tempting, too, every time you pass through the kitchen!)

6 apples, peeled and sliced
1½ cups whole cranberries
½ cup chopped nuts
1 teaspoon cinnamon
⅛ teaspoon salt
¾ cup white sugar, divided

½ cup brown sugar
2 eggs
½ teaspoon vanilla
½ cup butter, melted
1 cup all-purpose flour

Grease a 9-inch pie pan or 8-inch square pan. Layer apples in pan, alternating with cranberries. Sprinkle nuts, cinnamon, salt, and ¼ cup sugar over fruit. Mix together brown sugar, remaining ½ cup white sugar, eggs, vanilla, butter, and flour. Pour this mixture over apples and berries, spreading evenly to cover (mixture will run down through the fruit.) Bake in 325° oven for 45 minutes, or until knife inserted into the center comes out clean. Serves 4–8.

Savory Cape Cod Recipes & Sketches (New England)

Lemon Cake Pie

This recipe is over 60 years old. It is good!

Juice and grated rind of
   1 lemon
1¼ cups milk
1 cup sugar

2 heaping tablespoons flour
2 eggs, separated
1 tablespoon melted butter
1 (9-inch) pie crust, unbaked

Beat together all ingredients, except 2 egg whites that have been beaten stiff; fold in beaten egg whites. Pour into pie crust. Bake in 325°oven for 1 hour, or until done.

Oma's (Grandma's) Family Secrets (Iowa)

Lemon Meringue Pie

Lemon Meringue Pie

Everyone's favorite.

1 Pillsbury refrigerated pie crust	7 egg yolks, beaten (reserve
1⅔ cups sugar	6 whites)
7 level tablespoons cornstarch	2 tablespoons butter
¾ cup fresh or bottled lemon	1 teaspoon lemon extract
juice	1 teaspoon orange extract
1¼ cups water	

Bring pie crust to room temperature. Preheat oven to 375°. Place crust in a 9¾-inch pie plate; flute edges. Thoroughly prick crust with fork so no bubbles appear when baked. Bake 10–12 minutes, or until golden brown.

Combine sugar and cornstarch in a 1-quart glass measuring pitcher. In separate 2-cup glass measuring pitcher, combine lemon juice and water. Microwave liquid on HIGH for 3 minutes. Add hot liquid to sugar mixture; whisk thoroughly. Temper egg yolks by adding ¼ cup of lemon mixture to yolks, and mix well; add to remaining lemon mixture, and whisk. Microwave on HIGH 2–3 minutes, until thickened. Stir. (Should be glossy and bright yellow.) Add 1 more minute of cooking time if mixture is not completely thick. Add butter, lemon extract, and orange extract; stir well. Pour lemon mixture into baked pie shell.

MERINGUE:

6 reserved egg whites	1 cup sugar
1 level teaspoon baking powder	2 tablespoons light corn syrup
1 teaspoon lemon extract	

In an electric stand mixer, beat reserved egg whites on HIGH until they are frothy. Beat in baking powder and lemon extract. Slowly drizzle sugar into egg mixture while beating. Add corn syrup. Continue beating until mixture is stiff and glossy. Do not underbeat. Top pie with Meringue, being sure to cover completely. Brown pie in 375° oven for about 15 minutes, till browned. Do not refrigerate. Serves 8–10.

Favorites from the Lunch Bell (Virginia)

Old-Fashioned Egg Custard Pie

Brings back memories of grandma's house.

3 eggs, beaten
¾ cup sugar
¼ teaspoon salt
1 teaspoon vanilla

½ teaspoon ground nutmeg,
   plus additional for top
1½ cups milk, scalded
1 (9-inch) pie shell, unbaked

Combine eggs and sugar, beating well. Add salt, vanilla, and ½ teaspoon nutmeg. Gradually add scalded milk, stirring constantly. Pour mixture into pie shell, and sprinkle with additional nutmeg. Bake at 400° for 10 minutes; reduce heat to 325°, and bake an additional 25 minutes, or till knife comes out clean. Cool thoroughly before serving. Serves 6–8.

Favorite Recipes (Kentucky)

Praline Pie

This pie is incredible.

⅓ cup butter
⅓ cup packed brown sugar
½ cup chopped pecans
1 (3-ounce) box butterscotch
   pudding mix

1 (8-inch) pie crust, lightly baked
   (do not brown)
Whipped topping
Nuts for garnish

Cook and stir butter and sugar until sugar melts and it boils vigorously. Remove from heat. Add nuts. Pour into crust, and bake at 425° for 5 minutes (it will be bubbly). Meanwhile, prepare pudding as directed; cool, stirring twice. Spoon into crust. Chill. Serve with whipped topping. Garnish with nuts.

Editor's Extra: Use ¼ cup less milk than called for on pudding mix to have a better cutting pie.

Homemade with Love (West Virginia)

Blue Ribbon Cafe's Old-Fashioned Chocolate Cream Pie

Old classics are hard to beat.

CRUST:

1 cup all-purpose flour
½ teaspoon salt

⅓ cup shortening
2 tablespoons ice water

In bowl, combine flour and salt. Cut in shortening until mixture is consistency of coarse meal. Add ice water, 1 tablespoon at a time, until mixture stays together when formed into a ball. Roll out on floured board until about ⅛ inch thick. Place in 9-inch pie pan, and crimp around edges. Prick Crust several times with fork. Bake in 350° oven for 10–12 minutes. Set aside to cool.

FILLING AND MERINGUE:

2 cups evaporated milk
½ cup water
2¼ cups sugar, divided
3 tablespoons all-purpose flour
½ teaspoon salt

4 tablespoons cocoa
4 egg yolks, beaten
1 tablespoon butter
1 teaspoon vanilla
4 egg whites

In medium saucepan, combine evaporated milk and water. Bring to scalding (not boiling) point. In another bowl, combine 1½ cups sugar, flour, salt, and cocoa. Add egg yolks and mix into a thick batter. Add batter to milk-water mixture, stirring constantly with whisk. Cook over medium heat until thickened. Remove from heat, and add butter and vanilla, stirring well to blend. Pour into baked Crust, and allow to cool.

Prepare Meringue by beating egg whites at high speed in bowl until stiff. Add remaining ¾ cup sugar, and beat until peaks form. Top pie with Meringue. Bake in 350° oven for 6–8 minutes until top is golden brown. Cool and serve.

Arizona's Historic Restaurants and their Recipes (Arizona)

Marvelous Mocha Pie

Ridiculously delicious!

20 chocolate Oreo cookies,
  crushed

¼ cup butter, melted
1 quart coffee ice cream, softened

Combine well-crushed cookies with melted butter, and press into pie plate. Spread 1 full quart softened ice cream over crust, and freeze.

CHOCOLATE SAUCE:
3 (3-ounce) squares
  unsweetened chocolate
¼ cup butter

⅔ cup sugar
⅔ cup evaporated milk
1 teaspoon vanilla

Bring chocolate, butter, and sugar to a boil. Gradually add evaporated milk. Cook until thickened. Let cool; add vanilla. Spread over ice cream, and return to freezer until sauce sets.

TOPPING:
1 cup whipping cream,
  whipped
Kahlúa (optional)

Sliced or slivered almonds,
  toasted

Before serving, top with whipped cream. Drizzle a small amount of Kahlúa over whipped cream, if desired. Garnish with nuts.

Editor's Extra: Flavored sliced almonds are sold in small packages in the produce department. Plain or honey-roasted would be nice . . . and convenient.

Soupçon II (Illinois)

Families are the compass that guides us. They are the inspiration to reach great heights, and our comfort when we occasionally falter.
—Brad Henry

Blueberry Sky Pie

This pie is nothing less than AWESOME!

1 (8-ounce) package cream
  cheese, softened
6 ounces frozen lemonade
1 (14-ounce) can sweetened
  condensed milk

1 (21-ounce) can blueberry pie
  filling, divided
2 (8-inch) prepared graham
  cracker pie crusts

Beat cream cheese until creamy; add lemonade and condensed milk. Mix till well blended. Fold together ¾ of cream cheese mixture and ⅔ of pie filling. Spread into crusts; chill. Garnish with remaining cream cheese mixture and remaining pie filling. Makes 2 pies.

Culinary Classics (Georgia)

Frozen Key Lime Pie

Here's a pie that is always well-received at family gatherings—light, refreshing, and delicious!

½ cup lime juice
1 cup sweetened condensed milk
1 cup chopped pecans
1 (20-ounce) can crushed
  pineapple, drained

1 (16-ounce) carton Cool Whip
4–6 drops green food coloring
2 (8-inch) prepared graham
  cracker crusts

Mix together all ingredients, except crusts. Divide mixture evenly between crusts. Place in freezer to set. Keep frozen until ready to serve.

Let's ACT Up in the Kitchen (Florida)

Other things may change us, but we start and end with the family.

—Anthony Brandt

Butter Brickle Ice Cream Pie

Nothing beats a slice of ice cream pie on a hot summer day.

½ cup brown sugar
¼ cup butter
1 tablespoon water

4 cups cornflakes
½ gallon vanilla ice cream

In a saucepan, bring first 3 ingredients to a boil, stirring constantly. Pour over cornflakes in a large bowl. Spoon ⅔ of cornflake mixture into a 9-inch pie tin or plate, and press in the bottom and up sides. Soften ice cream by setting out for a brief time. Spread softened ice cream into cornflake-lined pie plate. When filled, spread remaining cornflake mixture over the top of ice cream, and freeze. Serves 8.

Cookin' in the Spa (Arkansas)

Oreo Cookie Pie

A make-ahead favorite. What's not to like?

1 (3-ounce) package vanilla
  instant pudding mix
1 cup water
1 (14-ounce) can sweetened
  condensed milk
1 (8-ounce) package cream
  cheese, softened

1 (12-ounce) container Cool
  Whip
Chocolate pie crust
6 Oreo cookies

Mix pudding mix, water, condensed milk, and cream cheese; add Cool Whip; mix well. Pour ½ into pie crust; reserve remainder. Crush Oreo cookies (not too small), and sprinkle on top of first layer, then spoon remaining filling on top. Refrigerate. Can freeze.

Barbara's Been Cookin' (Mississippi)

It sounds cliche, but success is your friends, your family, what you do, and if you're happy when you wake up.

—Michael Pitt

Orange Pineapple Sherbet

Wow . . . only three ingredients!

1 (2-liter) bottle Orange Crush
  soda
2 (14-ounce) cans condensed
  milk

1 (20-ounce) can crushed
  pineapple, undrained

Mix all ingredients. Pour into an ice cream maker, and turn. Turns into the creamiest sherbet you've ever tasted!

Hint: If you don't have an ice cream maker, you can halve the recipe (use a small can of pineapple). Put mixture into a stainless steel mixing bowl, and pop into freezer. It takes a bit longer, but it's great.

Fishin' for a Cure (Kentucky)

Homemade Butter-Pecan
Ice Cream

A popular flavor— and so good!

1 (14-ounce) can sweetened
  condensed milk
1 (12-ounce) can evaporated
  milk
1½ cups sugar

4 eggs, slightly beaten
1 (12-ounce) jar caramel topping
1 teaspoon butter flavoring
1 cup chopped pecans
Milk to fill freezer

Combine condensed milk, evaporated milk, sugar, and eggs in saucepan, stirring well. Cook over medium heat, stirring often, about 5 minutes, or till thermometer reaches 160°. Stir in caramel topping, butter flavoring, and pecans. Cool, if necessary. Pour mixture into freezer container of 1-gallon hand-turned or electric ice cream maker. Add milk as needed to reach the fill line. Freeze according to manufacturer's instructions.

Bountiful Blessings (Virginia)

Easy-Do Fresh Strawberry Mousse

Easy-Do Fresh Strawberry Mousse

A strawberry lover's delight.

1 pint ripe strawberries,
  hulled, cleaned, and dried
1 (3-ounce) package
  strawberry-flavored gelatin
1 cup boiling water
½ tablespoon lemon juice
¼ cup sugar
Pinch of salt
¼ cup strawberry liqueur or
  brandy (optional)

1 cup heavy cream
Additional sweetened, flavored
  whipped cream for garnish
Additional whole strawberries
  for garnish
Fresh mint sprigs for garnish
  (optional)

Slice strawberries, then coarsely mash with a potato masher (should be about 1½ cups); set aside. In small bowl, dissolve gelatin in boiling water. In large bowl, combine strawberries, lemon juice, sugar, and salt. Add dissolved gelatin and strawberry liqueur, if desired, mixing well. Chill until mixture is the consistency of unbeaten egg whites.

In a chilled small heavy bowl, beat cream with chilled beaters until stiff peaks form. Fold whipped cream into chilled gelatin mixture. Spoon into individual sherbet glasses or dessert cups, or a 1-quart mold; chill several hours until mousse is set. Garnish each serving with additional sweetened, flavored whipped cream, a whole strawberry, and a fresh mint sprig, if desired. Serves 4.

Variation: One pint fresh raspberries may be substituted. Purée and strain berries. Raspberry liqueur may be used.

More Richmond Receipts (Virginia)

Having a place to go—is a home. Having someone to love—is a family. Having both—is a blessing.
—Donna Hedge

Hot Brownie Pudding

Chocolate, rich, warm, and gooey—basically, perfection!

1 cup all-purpose flour
¼ teaspoon salt
¾ cup sugar
2 teaspoons baking powder
1½ teaspoons cocoa plus
  3 tablespoons, divided

½ cup milk
½ cup chopped nuts
2 tablespoons butter, melted
½ cup brown sugar
½ cup white sugar
1 cup water

Sift together flour, salt, sugar, baking powder, and 1½ teaspoons cocoa. Add milk, nuts, and butter. Pour into greased casserole dish.

Mix brown sugar, white sugar, remaining 3 tablespoons cocoa, and water. Pour over first mixture in casserole dish, and bake at 350° for 1 hour. Serve warm with ice cream or whipped cream.

Best Made Better Recipes, Volume II (Kentucky)

Tammi's Banana Pudding

Dessert in a hurry!

2 (14-ounce) cans sweetened
  condensed milk
3 cups cold water
2 (3½-ounce) packages French
  vanilla instant pudding mix

2 envelopes Dream Whip
1 cup milk
1 box vanilla wafers
6 bananas, sliced

Do not use mixer for this recipe. Combine condensed milk and water in large bowl. Add pudding mixes, and beat till thick. Chill 5 minutes.

In separate bowl, mix Dream Whip and milk by hand till blended, not whipped. Stir into chilled pudding mixture. Layer wafers, bananas, and pudding till all are used. Refrigerate.

Oeder Family & Friends Cookbook (Ohio)

Caramel Bread Pudding

This is an old recipe of my mother's. It is the fluffiest bread pudding I have ever eaten.

¾ cup light brown sugar,
  packed
3 slices buttered white, raisin,
  or whole-wheat bread, cut
  into ½-inch squares
3 large eggs

1 cup milk
Dash of salt
½ teaspoon vanilla
Ice cream, whipped cream, or
  plain cream

Generously butter inside of double boiler top; pour in brown sugar; then add bread squares. Beat eggs with milk, salt, and vanilla; pour over bread; do not stir. Cook over gently boiling water, 1 hour, making sure water does not boil out of lower pot. Serve warm with or without a pitcher of cream. Serves 4.

Variation: For chocolate pudding, melt 1 square chocolate in buttered double boiler top. Stir in brown sugar and ¼ cup milk. Cook over boiling water until sugar dissolves, then add rest of ingredients and remaining ¾ cup milk. Do not stir. Cook as in caramel recipe.

Raleigh House Cookbook II (Texas)

Old-Fashioned Bread Pudding

Pure comfort food at its best!

3 cups soft bread crumbs
  (4 cups for firmer pudding)
2 cups milk
¼ cup butter or margarine
½ cup sugar

2 eggs, slightly beaten
¼ teaspoon salt
½ teaspoon cinnamon
½ teaspoon nutmeg
½ cup raisins

Place bread crumbs in 1½-quart baking dish. Scald milk and butter together. Add to crumbs. Blend in sugar, eggs, salt, cinnamon, nutmeg, and raisins. Place baking dish in pan of water 1 inch deep. Bake at 350° for 40–45 minutes.

Variations: For chocolate bread pudding, use ½ cup chocolate chips—omit raisins and spices.

Favorite Recipes of Montana (Big Sky)

Tres Elegant
Chocolate Ice Box Dessert

This is a beautiful dessert. Serve it when only the best is good enough for your family.

2 dozen lady fingers
3 bars Baker's German's Sweet
  Chocolate
3 tablespoons sugar
3 tablespoons hot water
6 eggs, separated

1 cup ground pecans
¾ cup mini marshmallows
1 pint whipping cream, whipped
Red cherries and whole pecans
  for garnish

Lightly grease a springform pan. Split lady fingers; layer bottom of pan, breaking a few to fill up gaps. Stand lady fingers around pan, flat side facing out.

Heat chocolate, sugar, and hot water in top of a double boiler, stirring until melted and smooth. Remove from heat. Add egg yolks, 1 at a time, beating well after each addition. Cook till thick. Cool. Beat egg whites stiff, and fold into chocolate mixture. Add ground pecans and marshmallows. Pour into prepared springform pan. Refrigerate overnight.

When ready to serve, remove rim from springform pan. Put whipped cream on top of cake, and garnish with cherries and whole pecans. This cake freezes well, even with whipped cream on top.

Editor's Extra: Dark sweet chocolate can be subbed for German's Sweet Chocolate.

The Country Gourmet (Miriam G. Cohn) (Mississippi)

A mom's hug lasts long after she lets go.
—Author Unknown

*Tres Elegant
Chocolate Ice Box
Dessert*

Blueberry Icebox Dessert

You will sing its praises.

1½ cups graham cracker
  crumbs
½ cup confectioners' sugar
½ cup butter, melted
4 eggs, well beaten
2 cups sugar

2 (8-ounce) packages cream
  cheese, softened
1 (21-ounce) can blueberry pie
  filling
Juice of ½ lemon
Nondairy whipped topping

Preheat oven to 350°. Coat a 9x13-inch pan with nonstick cooking spray. In medium bowl, combine graham cracker crumbs, confectioners' sugar, and butter; pat mixture into pan to form a crust. In large bowl, blend eggs, sugar, and cream cheese together with an electric mixer until smooth. Spread mixture over crumb mixture. Bake about 30 minutes.

Mix pie filling with lemon juice, and pour over top of slightly cooled cake. Refrigerate until ready to serve. Top with whipped topping. Serves 6–8.

Recipe submitted by Cindy Larson of The Deweys
The Southern Gospel Music Cookbook (Tennessee)

Quick and Easy
Blackberry Cobbler

A summertime delight!

2 quarts blackberries
½ cup lemon juice
4 cups sugar

1 tablespoon butter
2 packages canned biscuits

Mash berries and add lemon juice, sugar, and butter. Bring to a boil, and reduce heat. Simmer 10 minutes or until berries change color and mixture thickens. Pour into buttered baking dish or a thin pie crust. Top hot berries with canned biscuits, just touching, and bake, following package directions for biscuits. This is usually 8–12 minutes at 400°–425°. Serve hot with whipped cream or vanilla ice cream.

The Wild and Free Cookbook (Washington)

Strawberry Pizza I

So pretty and good.

CRUST:

2 sticks butter, melted
2 cups all-purpose flour

1 cup chopped pecans

Combine ingredients, and spread in bottom of pizza pan. Bake at 350° for 20 minutes. Cool.

FILLING:

1 (8-ounce) package cream
   cheese, softened
1 cup confectioners' sugar
1 teaspoon vanilla

1 (16-ounce) container Cool
   Whip
2 pints strawberries, sliced

Mix cream cheese and powdered sugar together; add vanilla and Cool Whip. Layer Filling on top of cooled Crust. Spread strawberries over Filling, then Glaze.

GLAZE:

1 cup strawberries
1 cup water
½ cup sugar

2 tablespoons cornstarch
Cold water

Crush strawberries; add water; strain through sieve. Combine sugar with strawberry juice in saucepan; stir and heat to boiling. Mix cornstarch with small amount of cold water to form a paste. Add to boiling berry juice. Stir until thick. Cool; spoon carefully over strawberries. Refrigerate leftovers.

Strawberries: From Our Family's Field to Your Family's Table (Georgia)

Happiness is only real when shared.
—Mother Teresa

Old-Fashioned Strawberry Shortcake

Yea! The old-fashioned "biscuit" shortcake.

Pinch of salt	**Butter**
2 cups all-purpose flour	**1 (10-ounce) box frozen**
4 teaspoons baking powder	**strawberries, thawed**
1 tablespoon sugar	**Sugar to taste**
4 tablespoons shortening	**Heavy cream**
⅔–¾ cup milk	

Mix dry ingredients together. Work in shortening with fingertips. Add milk, and mix to a soft dough. Pat out on a slightly floured board. Cut with a large round cutter. Bake in 425° oven for 10–15 minutes. Split open while hot, and spread on a lot of butter. Pour crushed sweetened strawberries between layers and on top. Serve while warm with heavy cream. Serves 4–6.

Editor's Extra: Whether you whip the cream or not is a matter of preference.

Great Lakes Cookery (Michigan)

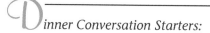

*D*inner Conversation Starters:

- *What musical artists do you admire the most?*

- *What would you most like to have, and rank them in preference: beauty, intelligence, or talent?*

- *What one thing would you most like to change about yourself?*

List of Contributors

Listed below are the cookbooks that have contributed recipes to the *Recipe Hall of Fame Family Favorites Cookbook*, along with copyright, author, publisher, city and state. The information in parentheses indicates the BEST OF THE BEST cookbook in which the recipe originally appeared.

All in Good Taste I ©1979 Service League Inc., Fond du Lac, WI (Wisconsin)

The Arizona Celebrity Cookbook ©1997 Eileen Bailey / Photos © Dand Leonard, Northland Publishing, Flagstaff, AZ (Arizona)

Arizona's Historic Restaurants and their Recipes ©1995 John F. Blair, Publisher, by Karen Surina Mulford, Winston-Salem, NC (Arizona)

Aromatherapy in the Kitchen ©2002 by Melissa Dale and Emmanuelle Lipsky, Woodland Publishing, Orem, UT (Utah)

The Authorized Texas Ranger Cookbook ©1994 Harris Farms Publishing, by Johnny and Cheryl Harris, Hamilton, TX (Texas)

The Bachelor's Cookbook ©1985 Dot Gibson Publications, Waycross, GA (Georgia)

Barbara's Been Cookin', by Barbara Buckley, Edwards, MS (Mississippi)

Best Made Better Recipes, Volume II, by Lincoln County 4-H Council, Stanford, KY (Kentucky)

Bethany's Best Bites, by Bethany Baptist Church, Andalusia, AL (Alabama)

Beyond Cotton Country ©1999 Junior League of Morgan County, Decatur, AL (Alabama)

Beyond the Grill ©1997 D.D. Publishing, by Debbye Dabbs, Madison, MS (Mississippi)

Bluegrass Winners ©1985 Garden Club of Lexington, KY (Kentucky)

Bountiful Blessings–Kenbridge Baptist Church ©1995 Morris Press Cookbooks, by Kenbridge Baptist Church, Kenbridge, VA (Virginia)

Breaking Bread Together, by Touching Hands, Meridian, MS (Mississippi)

Burnt Offerings II, by Jim Swindle, Columbia, TN (Tennessee)

Cajun Cuisine ©1985 Beau Bayou Publishing Co., Acadian House Publishing, Lafayette, LA (Louisiana)

Cakes . . . Cakes . . . and more Cakes, by Mariwyn McClain Smith, Parsons, WV (West Virginia)

Calvary's Cuisine, by Calvary Lutheran Church, Oroville, CA (California)

CASA Cooks, by CASA Foundation, Las Vegas, NV (Nevada)

A Century of Mormon Cookery, Volume I ©2002 Horizon Publishers & Distributors, Inc., by Hermine B. Horman, Bountiful, UT (Utah)

Children's Party Book ©1984 Junior League of Hampton Roads, Inc., Newport News, VA (Virginia)

Christ Reformed Church Historical Cookbook, by Christ Reformed Church, Martinsburg, WV (West Virginia)

Citrus Lovers Cook Book ©1980 Golden West Publishers, by Al and Mildred Fischer, Phoenix, AZ (Florida)

The Clovia Recipe Collection ©1996 Alumnae Association Beta of Clovia, Bloomington, MS (Minnesota)

A Collection of Recipes From St. Matthew Lutheran Church, by Rebecca Quilters, Galena, IL (Illinois)

Come and Discover Special Appetites, by Capital Area Down Syndrome Assn., Mason, MI (Michigan)

Comida Sabrosa ©1982 Irene Barraza Sanchez and Gloria Sanchez Yund, University of New Mexico Press, Albuquerque, NM (New Mexico)

Cook 'em Up Kaua'i ©1993 Kanuai Historical Society, Lihue, HI (Hawaii)

Cookin' in the Spa, by Hot Springs Junior Auxiliary, Hot Springs, AR (Arkansas)

Cookin' with the Colts, by Philip Barbour High School Marching Band, Philippi, WV (West Virginia)

The Cooking Book ©1978 The Junior League or Louisville, Inc., Louisville, KY (Kentucky)

Cooking with Kiwanis, by Kiwanis Club of Los Alamos, Santa Fe, NM (New Mexico)

Cooking with Miracle Deliverance ©2001 Miracle Deliverance Holiness Church, by Miracle Deliverance Mothers' Board, Columbia, SC (South Carolina)

Cooking with the Menno Haven Auxiliary, by Menno-Haven Auxiliary, Chambersburg, PA (Pennsylvania)

A Cook's Tour of Shreveport ©1964 The Junior League of Shreveport, Inc., Shreveport, LA (Louisiana)

Costco Wholesale Employee Association Cookbook, by Costco Employee Association, Kennewick, WA (Washington)

Country Classics II ©1997 Ginger Mitchell and Patsy Tompkins, Karval, CO (Colorado)

The Country Gourmet ©1978 Miriam H. Cohn, Alexandria, LA (Mississippi)

The Country Innkeepers' Cookbook ©1992 Wilf and Lois Copping, Country Roads Press, Castine, ME (New England)

Country Treasures, by Virginia Farm Bureau Kitchens, Richmond, VA (Virginia)

Culinary Classics, by Atlanta City Church's Creative Arts Dept., Fairburn, GA (Georgia)

Culinary Crinkles, by Presbyterian Women, Greenwood, SC (South Carolina)

Dawn to Dusk ©1998 Jonna Sigrist Cranebaugh, Olde World Bed & Breakfast, Dover, OH (Ohio)

Dd's Table Talk, by Deirdre Kieko Todd, Booklines Hawaii, Ltd., Mililani, HI (Hawaii)

Delightfully Seasoned Recipes, by Your 911 Family and Friends, Virginia Beach, VA (Virginia)

The Dexter Cider Mill Apple Cookbook ©1995 Katherine Merkel Koziski, Chelsea, MI (Michigan)

Dine with the Angels, by St. Michael's Catholic Youth, Henryetta, OK (Oklahoma)

Dinner Bell, by Lancaster County Society of Farm Women #22, Millersville, PA (Pennsylvania)

Dixie Dining ©1982 Mississippi Federation of Woman's Clubs, Inc., Jackson, MS (Mississippi)

Down Home Cooking from Hocking County, by Logan Hocking Chamber of Commerce, Logan, OH (Ohio)

Dude Food, by Jeannette Wilcox, Price, UT (Utah)

Dutch Pantry Cookin' Volume II, by Dutch Pantry Family Restaurant, Williamstown, WV (West Virginia)

Educated Taste, by LaGrange College Alumni Association, LaGrange, GA (Georgia)

Encore! Nashville ©1977 The Junior League of Nashville, Inc., Nashville, TN (Tennessee)

The Encyclopedia of Cajun and Creole Cuisine ©1983 The Encyclopedia Cookbook Committee, Inc., by Cuisine Promotions, Ltd., Baton Rouge, LA (Louisiana)

Fabulous Favorites, by Los Altos United Methodist Women, Los Altos, CA (California)

Family Favorites from the Heart, by Cheryl C. Huff, Springville, UT (Utah)

Family Secrets ©1986 Denise Wilson, Greenville, MS (Mississippi)

Famous Recipes from Mrs. Wilkes' Boarding House ©1976 Mrs. L.H. Wilkes, Savannah, GA (Georgia)

Favorite Island Cookery Book II, by Honpa Hongwanji Hawaii Betsuin, Honolulu, HI (Hawaii)

Favorite Recipes, by Nelson County Extension Homemakers, Bardstown, KY (Kentucky)

Favorite Recipes from First Church of God, by Women of the First Church of God, Gallipolis, OH (Ohio)

Favorite Recipes from the Heart of Amish Country, by Rachel Miller, Sugarcreek, OH (Ohio)

Favorite Recipes of Montana, by Montana Farm Bureau Federation Women's Committee, Bozeman, MT (Big Sky)

Favorite Utah Pioneer Recipes ©2000 Horizon Publishers & Distributors, Inc., by Marla Rawlings, Bountiful, UT (Utah)

Favorites from the Lunch Bell ©2010 by Betty Swain and The Lunch Bell, Newport News, VA (Virginia)

Feeding the Flock, by Meadow Fellowship Foursquare Church, Las Vegas, NV (Nevada)

The Fine Art of Dining, by Muscarelle Museum of Art, Williamsburg, VA (Virginia)

First Baptist Favorites, by First Baptist Church, Bisbee, AZ (Arizona)

Fishin' for a Cure ©2002 Mt. Carmel United Methodist Church, by Mt. Carmel Relay for Life, Benton, KY (Kentucky)

Five Loaves and Two Fishes II, by First United Methodist Church/United Methodist Women, Springfield, IL (Illinois)

Flavors ©1978 The Junior League of San Antonio, Inc., San Antonio, TX (Texas)

Four Seasons Cookbook ©1993 Avery Color Studios, by Bea Smith, Gwinn, MI (Michigan)

From Chaney Creek to the Chesapeake, by Family and Friends of Giles Dickenson Wise and Lenora Amburgery Wise, Virginia Beach, VA (Virginia)

From Our Home to Yours ©2003 by Lisa Shively Cookbooks, by Lisa Lofton Shively, Eden, NC (North Carolina)

Gibson/Goree Family Favorites, by Gibson/Goree Family of Choctaw County, Birmingham, AL (Alabama)

Gloriously Gluten-Free ©2011 Morris Press Cookbooks, by Karen A. Wilson, N.d., Woodbridge, VA (Virginia)

Golden Moments ©1996 by Arlene Giesel Koehn, Golden Moments Publishing, West Point, MS (Mississippi)

Gold'n Delicious ©1995 The Junior League of Spokane, WA (Washington)

Good Things to Eat, by Lynn Tritremmel, Hamilton, NJ (Mid-Atlantic)

Goodies and Guess-Whats ©1981 Helen Christiansen, Walsh, CO (Colorado)

Gourmet: The Quick and Easy Way, by Diana Allen, Enid, OK (Oklahoma)

Grannie Annie's Cookin' at the Homestead, by Ann Berg, Firewood Herb Garden and Gifts, Kenai, AK (Alaska)

Gran's Gems, by Jane Rayburn Hardin, Birmingham, AL (Mississippi)

The Great Cookbook ©1986 Altrusa Club of Greater Gadsden, Inc., Gadsden, AL (Alabama)

Great Lakes Cookery ©1991 Avery Color Studios, by Bea Smith, Gwinn, MI (Michigan)

Great Tastes of Texas ©1994 Barbara C. Jones, Bonham, TX (Texas)

Heart & Soul ©2001 Clinch Chapel United Methodist Church Youth Choir, White Oak, GA (Georgia)

Heart of the Harbor ©2009 Heart of the Harbor, by The Portsmouth Museums Foundation, Portsmouth, VA (Virginia)

Heart of the Home Recipes ©1980 Capper Press, Inc., Ogden Publications, Inc., Topeka, KS (Great Plains)

Heart Smart Kids Cookbook ©1996 Detroit Free Press, by Henry Ford Health System, Detroit, MI (Michigan)

Heavenly Recipes, by Milnor Lutheran Church WELCA, Milnor, ND (Great Plains)

Heavenly Recipes, by New Assembly Church, Beaver Dam, KY (Kentucky)

High Cotton Cookin' ©1978 Marvell Academy Mothers' Association, Marvell, AR (Arkansas)

Home at the Range II, by Chapter EX. P.E.O., Oakley, KS (Great Plains)

Home Made with Love, by St. John United Methodist Church, Owensboro, KY (Kentucky)

Homecoming ©1994 Baylor University Alumni Association, Waco, TX (Texas)

Homemade with Love, by Beverly Elementary, Beverly, WV (West Virginia)

If It Tastes Good, Who Cares? II ©1992 Spiritseekers Publishing, by Pam Girard, Bismark, ND (Great Plains)

It's Our Serve, by Junior League of Long Island, Roslyn, NY (New York)

Iuka Masonic Lodge Cookbook, by Iuka Masons, Iuka, MS (Mississippi)

Just for the Halibut ©1988 Flatfish Publications, by Nanci A. Morris, King Salmon, AK (Alaska)

Just Inn Time for Breakfast ©1992 Tracy M. Winters and Phyllis Y. Winters, Greensburg, IN (Michigan)

Kailua Cooks ©2002 Le Jardin Academy, Island Heritage Publishing, Kailua, HI (Hawaii)

Kay's Kitchen, by Kay Gundersen, Ketchikan, AK (Alaska)

Keepers ©1980 Helene Randolph Moore, New Braunfels, TX (Texas)

Kids in the Kitchen, by Parents Who Care, New Beginnings Child Development Center, Ft. Huachuca, AZ (Arizona)

Kinder Bakker ©1983 Junior Welfare League of Holland, MI (Michigan)

Koinonia Cooking ©1982 Elaine S. Mynatt, Knoxville, TN (Tennessee)

LaConner Palates ©1998 Patricia Flynn and Patricia McClane, Bookends Publishing, Oak Harbor, WA (Washington)

The Lady & Sons Just Desserts ©2002 by Paula H. Deen, Savannah, GA (Georgia)

The Lady & Sons, Too! ©2000 by Paula H. Deen, Savannah, GA (Georgia)

Let Me Serve You, by Carolyn Kay, Greenwood, SC (South Carolina)

Let's ACT Up in the Kitchen, by Abuse Counseling and Treatment, Inc., Fort Myers, FL (Florida)

Lion House Entertaining ©2003 Hotel Temple Square Corporations, Deseret Book Company, Salt Lake City, UT (Utah)

Little Bit Different! ©1979 St. John's Episcopal Church, Moultrie, GA (Georgia)

A Little Southwest Cookbook ©1993 Chronicle Books, by Barbara Karoff, San Francisco, CA (New Mexico)

Loaves and Fishes ©1984 The Episcopal Churchwomen, St. Paul's Episcopal Church, Daphne, AL (Alabama)

Look Who Came to Dinner ©2000 The Junior Auxiliary of Amory, MS, Inc., Amory, MS (Mississippi)

Louisiana Largesse ©1983 Capital City Press, by Baton Rouge Morning Advocate, Baton Rouge, LA (Louisiana)

Loving, Caring and Sharing, by Cordelia Higgins, Crewe, VA (Virginia)

Lutheran Church Women Cookbook, by Lutheran Church Women of Missouri Valley, Missouri Valley, IA (Iowa)

The Lymes' Heritage Cookbook ©1991 The Lyme Historical Society, Florence Griswold Museum, Old Lyme, CT (New England)

Mary B's Recipes, by Mary Anne Fritts, Burlington, NC (North Carolina)

Mennonite Country-Style Recipes & Kitchen Secrets ©1987 Herald Press, by Esther H. Shank, Scottdale, PA (Pennsylvania)

Miss Patti's Cook Book ©1997 Patti's Enterprises, by Chip Tullar, Grand Rivers, KY (Kentucky)

Montezuma Amish Mennonite Cookbook II, by Mrs. Ruth Yoder, Montezuma, GA (Georgia)

More Richmond Receipts ©1990 Jan Carlton, Norfolk, VA (Virginia)

Mountain Elegance ©1982 The Junior League of Asheville, Inc., Bright Mountain Books, Asheville, NC (North Carolina)

Mountain Recipe Collection ©1981 Ison Collectibles, Inc., by Valeria S. Ison, Hazard, KY (Kentucky)

Mrs. Rowe's Favorite Recipes, by Mike DiGrassi, Staunton, VA (Virginia)

Nashville Seasons ©1964 The Junior League of Nashville, Inc., Nashville, TN (Tennessee)

Never Trust a Skinny Chef...II, by Les Kincaid, Las Vegas, NV (Nevada)

90th Anniversary Trinity Lutheran Church Cookbook, by Trinity Ladies Fellowship, Great Bend, KS (Great Plains)

Oeder Family & Friends Cookbook, by Dianna Browning, Lebanon, OH (Ohio)

Of Pots and Pipkins ©1971 The Junior League of Roanake Valley, Inc., Roanoke, VA (Virginia)

Oma's (Grandma's) Family Secrets, by Linda F. Selzer, Homestead, IA (Iowa)

101 Things To Do With a Cake Mix ©2002 by Stephanie Ashcraft, Gibbs Smith, Publisher, Layton, UT (Utah)

101 Things To Do With a Slow Cooker ©2003 by Stephanie Ashcraft and Janet Eyring, Gibbs Smith, Publisher, Layton, UT (Utah)

Onions Make the Meal Cookbook, by Idaho-Eastern Oregon Onion Committee, Parma, ID (Idaho)

Our Best Home Cooking, by Vienna Baptist Church (West Virginia)

Our Daily Bread, by Fellowship Memorial Baptist Ladies Aid Society, Oak Hill, WV (West Virginia)

Our Lady of Mercy Church Recipes, by Lady of Mercy Church, Rochester, NY (New York)

Peanut Palate Pleasers from Portales, by Portales Woman's Club, Portales, NM (New Mexico)

Philadelphia Homestyle Cookbook ©1984 Norwood-Fontbonne Home and School Assn., Philadelphia, PA (Pennsylvania)

A Pinch of Rose & A Cup of Charm ©1998 by Rose Dorchuck, Kosciusko, MS (Mississippi)

Popus-An Island Tradition ©1995 The Bess Press, Inc., by Sachi Fukuda, Honolulu, HI (Hawaii)

Provisions & Politics ©2003 James K. Polk Memorial Association, Columbia, TN (Tennessee)

Quick Crockery Cooking ©1997 Cyndi Duncan and Georgie Patrick, C & G Publishing, Inc., Greeley, CO (Colorado)

Raleigh House Cookbook II ©1995 Raleigh House, by Martha R. Johnson, Kerrville, TX (Texas)

Recipes & Remembrances ©2004 Morris Press Cookbooks, by Arab First United Methodist Church, Arab, AL (Alabama)

Recipes from the Heart, by St. Mark Lutheran Church and Preschool, Elko, NV (Nevada)

Recipes from the Kitchens of Family & Friends, by Bahari Court #104, Ladies Oriental Shrine of North America, Winston, OR (Oregon)

Recipes of the Durbin, by Mary Durbin, Homer, IN (Indiana)

Recipes Tried and True, by Diana Swift, Wapiti Meadow Ranch, Cascade, ID (Idaho)

Red Flannel Town Recipes, by Red Flannel Festival, Cedar Springs, MI (Michigan)

Red River Valley Potato Growers Auxiliary Cookbook, by R.R.V.P.G. Auxiliary, East Grand Forks, MN (Great Plains)

Remembering the Past—Planning for the Future, by Lawson United Methodist Church, Lawson, MO (Missouri)

The Route 66 Cookbook ©1993 Marian Clark, Council Oak Books, Ltd., Tulsa, OK (Oklahoma)

RSVP ©1982 The Junior League of Portland, ME, Inc., Portland, ME (New England)

A Samford Celebration Cookbook, by Samford University Auxiliary, Birmingham, AL (Alabama)

Sand in My Shoes ©1990 by Jeannine B. Browning, Melbourne, FL (Florida)

Savor Summerville, by Linda McCoy, Summerville, SC (South Carolina)

Savory Cape Cod Recipes & Sketches ©1992 Gail Cavaliere, North Eastham, MA (New England)

Sensational Seafood Recipes and More! ©2007 Morris Press Cookbooks, by Great Bridge Fisherman's Association, Chesapeake, VA (Virginia)

Sharing Our Best ©1996 Eagle Historical Society & Museums, Eagle, AK (Alaska)

Sharing Our Best, by St. Paul's Lutheran Church, Saratoga Springs, NY (New York)

Sharing Our Best ©2002 Franklin Community Church, by Apples of Gold Women's Ministry of Franklin Community Church, Franklin, TN (Tennessee)

Sharing Our Best, by Bergen Lutheran Church, Montevideo, MN (Minnesota)

Sing for Your Supper, by Warsaw Presbyterian Church Choir, Warsaw, NC (North Carolina)

Sister's Secrets, by Beta Sigma Phi, Ville Platte, LA (Louisiana)

The Smithfield Cookbook ©1978 The Junior Woman's Club of Smithfield, VA (Virginia)

Smyth County Extension Homemakers Cookbook, by the Smyth County Extension Homemakers, Marion, VA (Virginia)

Soupçon II ©1982 The Junior League of Chicago, Inc., Chicago, IL (Illinois)

The Southern Gospel Music Cookbook ©1998 Bethni Hemphill, Brenda McClain, Ken Beck, and Jim Clark , Cumberland House Publishing, Nashville, TN (Tennessee)

Southern Sideboards ©1978 Junior League of Jackson, JLJ Publications, Jackson, MS (Mississippi)

Southern Spice à la Microwave ©1980 Margie Brignac, Pelican Publishing Company, Gretna, LA (Louisiana)

Stir Crazy! ©1986 Junior Welfare League of Florence, SC (South Carolina)

The Stirling City Hotel Favorite Recipes, by Charlotte Ann Hilgeman / Illustrated by Linda Hilgeman, Stirling City, CA (California)

Strawberries: From Our Family's Field to Your Family's Table ©2005 Calhoun Produce, Inc., Ashburn, GA (Georgia)

Summertime Treats ©1999 Sara Perry, Chronicles Books, San Francisco, CA (Oregon)

The Sun and the Rain & the Appleseed ©2011 by First Presbyterian Preschool, Richmond, VA (Virginia)

Sun-Sensational Southern Cuisine, by Sun-Sations Tanning Salon and Spa, Inc., Waxhaw, NC (North Carolina)

Take Two & Butter 'Em While They're Hot! ©1998 Native Ground Music, Inc., by Barbara Swell, Asheville, NC (West Virginia)

Taste & See, by Women Ministries of Sardinia Baptist, Westport, IN (Indiana)

Taste Buds ©1985 Winslow, Woverton, and Komegay, Hertford, NC (North Carolina)

Taste of Clarkston: Tried & True Recipes, by Clarkston Area Chamber of Commerce, Clarkston, MI (Michigan)

A Taste of Fishers ©1993 Fishers Tri Kappa, Fishers, IN (Indiana)

A Taste of Salt Air & Island Kitchens, by Ladies Auxiliary of the Block Island Volunteer Fire Department, Block Island, RI (New England)

A Taste Through Time, by Woodruff Community Center, Woodruff, SC (South Carolina)

Tastes from the Country, by Medicine Mt. Grange, Medimont, ID (Idaho)

Tennessee Homecoming: Famous Parties, People & Places ©1981 Phila Hach, Clarksville, TN (Tennessee)

Texas Accents ©1990 The Cancer Research Foundation of North Texas, Arlington, TX (Texas)

A Texas Hill Country Cookbook ©1976 Blue Lake—Deerhaven Cookbook Committee, San Antonio, TX (Texas)

Tiger Bait' Recipes ©1976 LSU Alumni Federation, Baton Rouge, LA (Louisiana)

Treasured Recipes, by Snowdoun United Methodist Women, Montgomery, AL (Alabama)

Treasures from Our Kitchen ©2001 United Methodist Women, Waynesboro, MS (Mississippi)

Truly Montana Cookbook ©2002 Bitterroot Valley Public Television, Hamilton, MT (Big Sky)

Tumm Yummies, by Y-Wives, Tiffin, OH (Ohio)

Turnip Greens in the Bathtub ©1981 Genie Taylor Harrison, Baton Rouge, LA (Louisiana)

Upper Kenai River Inn Breakfast Cookbook, by Peggy J. Givens, Upper Kenai River Inn, Cooper Landing, AK (Alaska)

Vaer saa god Cookbook, by WELCA St. John's Lutheran Church, Springfield, MN (Minnesota)

Victorian Sampler ©1986 Jim and Ruth Spears, Eureka Springs, AR (Arkansas)

Village Royale: Our Favorite Recipes, by Nancy Carden, Boynton Beach, FL (Florida)

Visitation Parish Cookbook, by St. Rita's Circle of Visitation Parish, Stacyville, IA (Iowa)

What's Cookin' ©1993 Arlene Luskin, Goodyear, AZ (Mid-Atlantic)

Where There's a Will... ©1997 Evelyn Will, Easton, MS (Mid-Atlantic)

T*he Wild and Free Cookbook* ©1996 Tom Squier, Breakout Productions/Loompanics Unlimited, Port Townsend, WA (Washington)

Winners ©1985 The Junior League of Indianapolis, Inc., Indianapolis, IN (Indiana)

Winnehaha's Favorite Recipes, by Winnehaha's of Minnesota, Circle Pines, MN (Minnesota)

With Hands & Heart Cookbook ©1990 Bethesda General Hospital Woman's Board, St. Louis, MO (Missouri)

Words Worth Eating ©1987 Jacquelyn G. Legg, Newport News, VA (Virginia)

Crab Cakes
page 114

Index

The Quest for the Best

The story of how two ladies,

Gwen McKee and Barbara Moseley,

went out to find America's best recipes,
and in the process, created the

BEST OF THE BEST STATE COOKBOOK SERIES

The process began in the early 1980s. After being involved in the development and publication of numerous cookbooks, Gwen McKee and Barbara Moseley were frequently asked what were their favorite cookbooks and recipes. From their own cookbook collections, they had highlighted recipes they thought were special. From this, the idea was born, "Why not collect all those highlighted recipes from different cookbooks into one cookbook?" They quickly realized that this ambitious undertaking could best be accomplished on a state-by-state basis. The BEST OF THE BEST STATE COOKBOOK SERIES had begun!

From the very beginning, Gwen and Barbara established goals. They would search for cookbooks that showcased recipes that captured local flavor. They would insist on kitchen-friendly recipes that anybody anywhere could cook and enjoy. They would make the books user friendly, and edit for utmost clarity.

The criteria for including a recipe was that it have three distinguishing features: *great taste, great taste, and great taste!*

In 1982, *Best of the Best from Mississippi: Selected Recipes from Mississippi's Favorite Cookbooks* was published. It was an immediate success and prompted going next door to Louisiana, Gwen's native state. The Louisiana edition, published in 1984, has been reprinted twenty-four times and is the best seller of all the states.

The two editors then took on Texas—four trips were required just to cover the territory! But cover it they did, selecting ninety-four cookbooks from all over Texas to contribute their most popular recipes to *Best of the Best from Texas Cookbook*. At 356 pages and over 500 recipes, Texas is still one of the largest cookbooks in the Series.

With three states under their belts, Gwen and Barbara now had a mission and a motto: ***Preserving America's Food Heritage***. The editors committed themselves to tracking down those classic family recipes that have been refined and perfected over generations. It had become an interesting, sometimes fascinating, often exhilarating process . . . and they knew they were hooked on wanting to explore each state and taste their cuisine.

Talking to townfolk was always fun and informative. Gwen and Barbara would usually be directed to someone else if that person couldn't help them—"Go see Sarah at the drugstore; she has lots of cookbooks."

Over the next four years, Gwen and

Barbara concentrated on those neighboring states that were convenient to get to. In the early days before the Internet, their normal method of finding local cookbooks was to travel throughout the state. Gwen usually did the driving, and Barbara—with map in lap—the navigating. They stopped at bookstores, gift and kitchen shops, chamber of commerce offices, tourist bureaus, and any other place that might offer the possibility of discovering a popular local cookbook. Without fail, in every state, the best thing was the people they met and the information they so proudly shared.

. . . We're covering the South!
1986–1990

Throughout the '90s, Gwen and Barbara continued to search with renewed dedication to finding and preserving those little recipe gems that might be tucked away in a modest church cookbook published in a small community. Junior League cookbooks, because they are developed by local members and contain recipes from their city and community, have been a particularly valuable contributor to the Series.

In addition to the over 300 wonderful recipes that each Best cookbook con-

Tasting the local fare is one of the best bonuses of a trip through any region in search of great recipes. In Hurricane Mills, Tennessee, Gwen and Barbara visited Loretta Lynn's Kitchen and found tasty local vittles and recipes.

each state. These are fun and informative, and help to convey the unique features of the state.

Each cookbook contains photographs and illustrations that capture some of the visual highlights of each state.

In the late '90s, the editors finished the Midwest and set their sites on the "big" states of the West. These states with their vast areas provided major challenges to locating those local cookbooks that might contain that special recipe.

In the Southwest, the *Arizona* and *New Mexico* editions became instant favorites. The popularity of the Mexican influence on the cuisine of this region, abundantly represented in these

tains, Gwen and Barbara have added other features that make the cookbooks more useful and enjoyable.

"Editor's Extras" have occasionally been added to the original recipes to ensure complete understanding, suggest an alternate ingredient if the original was not available, or offer an embellishment or variation the editors particularly liked and wanted to share.

Sprinkled throughout each BEST cookbook is a series of short "quips" that provide interesting facts about

. . . We're halfway there! 1991–1996

Hot Cheese in a Jar

2 pounds Velveeta cheese, melted
1 medium onion, grated
1 (5.33-ounce) can evaporated milk
1 pint Miracle Whip salad dressing
1 (8-ounce) can seeded, deveined
  jalapeño peppers, chopped fine
  (cut off stems)

Melt cheese in top of double boiler. Add onion, milk, Miracle Whip, and peppers to melted cheese, and mix well. Pour into 6 (8-ounce) jelly jars. Cool, screw on caps, and refrigerate.

This recipe was often made before road trips and a supply taken along. Many times the editors relied on this treat to make it through some long days of travel. The recipe was contributed by Cowtown Cuisine and is included in Best of the Best from Texas Cookbook *(page 28). It is truly a classic.*

cookbooks, surely contributed to their appeal.

The *California* edition, like *Texas* and *New England*, required more pages to accommodate the large number of contributing cookbooks. The great variety of recipes selected makes these cookbooks particularly interesting and enjoyable to use.

Gwen and Barbara knew from the beginning that they did not want the BEST OF THE BEST cookbooks to be hardbound, oversized, expensive books that would stay on the coffee table and not be allowed to go in the kitchen. They preferred a ringbound format that would allow for convenient lay-flat usage.

In 2000, after nearly two decades, Gwen and Barbara were still going strong. They had completed thirty-six states, had met many delightful people, had seen a great portion of their beautiful country, and were even more committed to their goal of *Preserving America's Food Heritage.*

Seattle's Pike Place Market was an exciting experience. The great variety of vegetables, fruits, and fish on display challenged the editors to find recipes that could fully exploit such an abundance of fresh ingredients. They feel they have met the challenge with Best of the Best from Washington Cookbook.

. . . We're almost there!
1997–2000

Gwen and Barbara greeted the new millennium with continued enthusiasm and dedication. They completed the remaining five states in the east, three of which (New Jersey, Delaware, and Maryland) were combined in the *Best of the Best from Mid-Atlantic* edition.

Now it was time to gear-up for the final push. They knew they would be a long way from home as they pursued recipes in the Northwest, Alaska, and Hawaii.

Oregon's fruit-growing district, "The Fruit Loop," offered many fresh fruit treats that inspired recipes like Boysenberry Swirl Cheesecake with Hazelnut Crust (*Best of the Best from Oregon Cookbook*, page 212).

The state fair in Palmer, Alaska, was another unique occasion to taste some local fare. The exhibit at the fair contained remarkable blue-ribbon winning fruits and vegetables.

In beautiful Hawaii, the editors encountered many helpful people, particularly Faith in Kauai who allowed the editors to review her own extensive cookbook collection, many of which were of a vintage nature. As with other states, the cookbook distributors were most helpful in bringing many local cookbooks to the attention of the editors. This was particularly true with Booklines in Hawaii and Todd Communications in Alaska.

Utah and Nevada, the final two states, offered an opportunity for the editors to experience not only the tasteful cuisine but also the unique beauty of the desert, quite different from their lush, green, southern landscapes.

When the final states were completed, and copies of *Best of the Best from Utah* and *Best of the Best from Nevada* cookbooks arrived from the printer, there was a great celebration at the Quail Ridge Press offices.

Now that the SERIES has been completed, what next? Gwen and Barbara, both grandmothers many times over, are not ready to retire. "There are still cookbooks to be discovered and tasteful recipes to be preserved," says Barbara, ". . . we might just start over."

"Regardless of what we do in the future," Gwen adds, "we set out to collect, and celebrate the food of America on a state-by-state basis, and that mission has been accomplished."

We did it!
2005

THE RECIPE HALL OF FAME COOKBOOK SERIES

Having completed their mission of preserving America's food heritage on a state-by-state basis, Gwen and Barbara indeed did not retire. Instead they began to search their database of over 25,000 favorite recipes collected from throughout America to find THE BEST of the Best of the Best! This collection would be called the RECIPE HALL OF FAME COOKBOOK SERIES. For this *Family Favorites Cookbook*, they concentrated

Barbara and Gwen relaxing after completing their first mission, before compiling the RECIPE HALL OF FAME COOKBOOK SERIES.

their focus on those "go-to" dishes that anchor the meal, the kind that always create exciting anticipation whenever they are served. This RECIPE HALL OF FAME cookbook, like its eight companion volumes, is all about great taste.

Q QUAIL RIDGE PRESS • www.quailridge.com